FOR GOODNESS' SAKE:

An Eating Well Guide
to Creative Low-Fat Cooking

By Terry Joyce Blonder

CAMDEN
◆HOUSE◆
PUBLISHING

Camden House Publishing, Inc.
A division of Telemedia Communications (USA) Inc.

Photographic properties courtesy of:

The Squeeze—platter, planter, and glasses: La Cache, Kingston, Ontario. **Lemon Rosemary Chicken**—plates and bowl: Kitchen Cargo, Kingston, Ontario. **More Than Apple Pie**—cooling rack and spoon: La Cache, Kingston, Ontario. **Oriental Chicken in Parchment**—plates, bowl, cup, and saucer: Kitchen Cargo, Kingston, Ontario. **Current Currant Carrot Cake**—bowl: Stokes, Kingston, Ontario. **Assorted Muffins**—baskets: Handmade Willow Baskets by Jule Koch, Clarendon, Ontario; bowls: Wilton Pottery, Wilton, Ontario. **Sunburst Salad**—platter: Stokes, Kingston, Ontario. **Four Peppers and Salmon Over Pasta**—plates, cup, saucer, and cutlery: Stokes, Kingston, Ontario; eucalyptus: Staples, Newburgh, Ontario. **Bean Enchiladas**—wine decanter and cups: Wilton Pottery, Wilton, Ontario. **Dressed Asparagus**—casserole, tureen, and cup: Kitchen Cargo, Kingston, Ontario. **Chinese Dumpling Rolls**—copper: La Cache, Kingston, Ontario. **Poached Pears in Raspberry Sauce**—plates and teapot: Stokes, Kingston, Ontario; napkin: La Cache, Kingston, Ontario. **Mixed Cookies and Squares**—plates, teapot, and mugs: Wilton Pottery, Wilton, Ontario. **Melon-Berry Swirl**—plate and bowl: Stokes, Kingston, Ontario.

Special thanks for assistance to: Glenn E. Auglin, The Fish House (Kingston, Ontario), Jane Good, Dat Lee Hong, Mitchell Kelsey, J. Shirley Menyes, Robin Morrin, Virginia Thompson

Camden House Publishing, Inc.
Ferry Road
Charlotte, Vermont 05445
A division of Telemedia Communications (USA) Inc.

First Edition

ISBN 0-944475-08-6

Library of Congress Catalogue Card Number: 90-083425

Edited by Sandra J. Taylor
Designed by Ann Aspell
Black and white illustrations by Joan Dunning
Inside color photography by Ernie Sparks

Trade distribution by
Firefly Books Ltd.
250 Sparks Avenue
Willowdale, Ontario
Canada M2H 2S4

Printed and bound in Canada by
D. W. Friesen & Sons
Altona, Manitoba

Cover recipe: Lemon Thyme Chicken Rolls, page 88

Contents

INTRODUCTION

◆

My first professional cooking job was as a chef in a low-fat health spa, where the only oil in the kitchen was the inedible type used on the knife-sharpening stone. The food there lived up to health claims, and after a month of dieting and exercise, the customers went home with healthier blood tests and fitter bodies.

The food met other expectations as well. No one expected it to taste as good as the food in the outside world, and, with few exceptions, it didn't. This experience caused me to question whether it was really necessary to choose between being a martyr for health or living the shortened life of an unhealthy hedonist. I wanted to find out when a healthful diet ceases to make sense and becomes unnecessary extremism. I wanted to find out why some low-fat recipes taste wonderful while others are failures.

I turned to the chemistry of food for answers. I learned which foods enhance flavors and which ones mellow them. I learned how foods interact with one another, and what happens when they hit the taste buds. I discovered what happens when food cooks and how temperature affects the changes.

I took a close look at oils and fats to learn when they are interchangeable, when they can be reduced, and when they are not needed at all.

I studied nutrition and learned which diet trends are based on fact and which have distorted the results of minor scientific studies. I examined some diets that addressed one health issue while ignoring others, and I researched diets based exclusively on philosophy instead of scientific fact.

During my investigation, I taught low-fat cooking classes and learned from my students, who impressed upon me their need for a relaxed, commonsense approach to a healthful diet. They wanted to understand enough about nutrition to make the right choices and not be misled by erroneous claims and fads; they wanted to learn an approach that was consistent but not tedious. They wanted fun, creative, time-saving recipes that were also good as leftovers.

Consequently, my cooking style and food philosophy began to develop along those lines, resulting in recipes that fit within the generally accepted guidelines for a low-fat, high-fiber, complex-carbohydrate diet. I impose certain restrictions, but all are nutritionally sound and none are hard on the chef. For example, I do not believe in using artificial ingredients or imitation foods for they never satisfy as the originals do. I do not try to copy cream sauces or use synthetic sugars or fake cheeses. There are plenty of fresh, minimally processed foods that can be eaten with far more gratifying results.

I want foods to be visually attractive, with clear flavors and appealing textures. I prefer creative recipes, not exotic ones. Precious foods aren't my style, and although extravagant ingredients can be fun at times, they are not my daily fare.

I love to cook, but I don't like fussy recipes. I like to cut and chop and watch the food simmer in a pan, but I don't want to worry over a difficult sauce, or take hours to prepare a meal that serves only two and doesn't leave leftovers.

The recipes included here have been taught to my students, have inspired many to cook who had once avoided the kitchen, and have encouraged others to invent their own recipes. I hope they will do the same for you.

Using This Book

The way a recipe is written makes a big difference once you begin working from it. I've tried to organize mine so they are easy to understand and follow. Ingredients are listed in the order in which they are used. Preparation instructions, such as ways to cut the vegetables, are next to the measurements so that everything is ready before you start combining the ingredients. The directions have numbered steps to help you keep your place.

Food, thankfully, does not come in perfect geometric packages. Because there are variations in size, flavor, and freshness, it is important that you follow your nose and your palate as well as my directions. I wrote these recipes as carefully as possible, giving attention to detail and incorporating suggestions made by recipe testers and students in my cooking classes.

We all have different tastes, so if, for example, you aren't as fond of garlic as I am, feel free to reduce the suggested quantity. The exception here is with baked goods, for which exact measurements are required and appropriate measuring tools are necessary. For flours, use measuring cups that can be leveled off at the tops; for liquids, use clear, marked cups of plastic or glass that allow for easy pouring.

Herbs are identified as dried or fresh. If you have access to fresh herbs, do use them. In most cases, it takes three times as much of the fresh to equal the effect of the concentrated dry. (Think how much sweeter raisins are than grapes, if you find this ratio hard to believe.)

I occasionally include a few unusual ingredients. These are fully explained either in the beginning of the book or next to the recipe in which they are used. They are not hard to work with, and I hope that unfamiliar foods will not keep you from trying the recipes.

I do not include preparation times for the recipes, because everyone works at different speeds and with different equipment. Cooking times are as accurate as possible. Because I cook with gas, I can get a high temperature immediately and adjust the flame to exactly where I want it. Electric stoves take longer to respond when the heat is reduced or increased.

Pots and pans also affect a recipe's outcome. Each retains heat differently. The thickness of their bottoms and the materials from which they are made determine whether a recipe heats evenly, burns, or scorches. Foods cooked in nonstick pans have a texture that is different from those cooked in oil. In addition, the larger the pan, the more liquid is needed for sautéing, and the quicker a sauce cooks down. Therefore, use your judgment when following these recipes.

The serving size or yield of a recipe is another variable, for not everyone uses the same size portions. (I, for example, consider 1½ cups of green beans to be a single serving.) Amounts also change according to whether the recipe is used as an appetizer, as the main dish, or as a side dish.

I want more than clear and concise recipes from a cookbook, however; I want to learn the whys behind the recipes. Understanding the chemical interactions among ingredients and how cooking techniques work, demystifying ethnic foods, and having a solid grasp of the basics make me a better cook (and satisfy my curiosity). Once I understand why a recipe works, I can successfully repeat it, or create a new one.

I include much of this information here. Some of it is placed in the introductory section of the book, and some is found in boxes next to the appropriate recipes. The index will help you find these details, and I hope this format makes the information more accessible and less intimidating. You certainly don't have to read it all before you start cooking, but I do hope you will read it eventually.

The success of these recipes relies heavily on using only the best ingredients available, whether that means finding the freshest, most flavorful vegetables, or buying the thickest and richest brand of canned tomatoes. With low-fat recipes, the flavors of the basic ingredients come through and make all the difference.

As my grandmother used to say, "With the best ingredients, how could it be bad?" and I add to that, "With the right knowledge, how could it go wrong?"

What Are the Limits?

◆

By now most of you know that what you eat affects your health, although there is still some confusion as to exactly what the best diet is. Contributing to this are well-publicized fads and diets that address only one health issue while ignoring the others. To make matters even worse, health-care professionals continue to disagree, so you also have to decide which expert to believe. In addition, as new research becomes available, nutritionists revise their thinking, which means that no conclusions can be considered as absolute.

Fortunately, there is a growing consensus among those in the medical community regarding the basics of a healthy diet. They concur that reducing fat, especially saturated fat, and increasing the consumption of complex, or minimally processed, carbohydrates (which provide fiber and nutrients) are essential when combating the health problems of the twentieth— soon to be twenty-first—century. They all agree that fruits and vegetables are a major component of a healthful diet, that protein should be eaten in moderation, and that salt and simple sugars should be kept to a minimum.

But the specifics are harder to pin down. Fifteen years ago, Nathan Pritikin was considered a radical when he espoused a 10% fat diet. Today, even those experts who suggest reducing fat to 30% of caloric intake admit that 20% might be better. Pritikin may have been an extremist, but he wasn't as far off base as some people thought.

All the uncertainty surrounding the "perfect" diet, along with the many fads around today, could make you believe that, as long as you eat moderately, you'll be fine. Unfortunately, the average American's daily fare is hardly healthy. A typical individual derives up to 40% of his or her calories from fat, and most of that fat is saturated (the worst type). The rest of the day's calories generally come from processed foods that are low in fiber and nutrients, and high in salt, cholesterol, and additives, hardly the basis for a healthful diet.

There is, however, a way to eat that is good for you, simple, and neither extreme nor fanatical. Unlike those of us in the United States, citizens of many other countries base their diets on beans, grains, vegetables, fruits, and small quantities of meat. By following this model, you will have a healthful diet.

Still, the specifics are elusive. How much olive oil? Should you use butter, salt, margarine? What about eggs, white pasta, avocados?

In deciding what to include in (and exclude from) this cookbook, I made decisions based both on my study of nutrition and on my experience as a chef. No diet works if you can't stay on it, but it also doesn't work if the nutritional benefits are compromised. So I chose to be as strict with these recipes as good taste would allow.

Fat is the most important thing to watch. It is high in calories and linked to heart disease, cancer, and obesity (among other ailments). As a general guideline, I keep the fat in meals to 25% or less of the total calories. Keeping in mind that a fat-free vegetable side dish will balance out an entrée made with oil, I occasionally allow my recipes to be more than 25% fat but rarely more than 40%.

Sometimes, however, calculating the percentage of fat does not accurately portray how healthful a recipe is. If a dish, such as a vegetable salad, is low in calories, the dressing may well be more than 40% of the calories, even if it contributes only a few grams of fat to the recipe. Or a cake recipe that is high in calories may be only 30% fat but still contribute 12 grams or more of fat.

Also, labels state grams of fat, not fat as a percentage of calories, so it is useful to know how many grams of fat should be consumed in a day.

A good and achievable goal, as stated above, is to take in less than 30% of your total daily calories from fat. To convert that to grams, first figure out how many calories your body needs to maintain itself. Because each pound of body weight requires 15 calories, simply multiply your desired weight by 15. (For example, a 120-pound person needs 1,800 calories.) Next, multiply that figure by 30% to get the maximum number of calories that should come from fat (in this example, 540). Since each gram of fat has 9 calories, divide fat calories by 9 to get the number of grams you should take in each day (in this case, 60). Now that I've explained the basics, I want to give you a simpler way to compute this. Divide your desired body weight by 2 to get the maximum number of grams of fat you may consume each day.

The recipes in this book have grams of fat listed to help you estimate your daily fat intake. But I've not only reduced total fat, I've also severely cut back on saturated fats, such as butter. (Saturated fats are the ones implicated in heart disease.) I even exclude margarine because it, too, is partially saturated. And except for the expensive margarines found in health food stores, they all have artificial colors and flavors. Even though these additives may not be a huge health risk, why take a chance?

The fats I include in this book come from oils (see page 25) and occasionally from nuts, low-fat dairy products, and small quantities of cheese.

Dairy products are an important source of calcium, protein, and vitamins, and the low-fat forms are essential for most people. Skim milk, low-fat yogurt and cottage cheese, farmer's cheese, and buttermilk are all lower in fat and can be used freely. Their quality varies, so sample a few brands in your area to find the ones you like best.

Most other cheeses are high in saturated fat and cholesterol, but occasionally I use a small amount if the recipe needs the flavor and texture, and if I can still keep the total fat content within an acceptable range.

There are few truly low-fat cheeses on the market, and even fewer that are worth eating. Be wary, too, of the supposedly reduced-fat cheeses that are sold. Some manufacturers list a ridiculously small portion size so that the fat content seems low, or they list fat by percentage of weight rather than of calories. As a general rule, if the fat content is more than 3 grams per ounce (check the nutritional labeling on the package), then it is not really low in fat.

High-fat foods that I do use are nuts, which can be from 60% to 90% fat. But nuts, like avocados, which I also eat, are low in saturated fats. They add flavor and texture to foods, and are a terrific source of protein, minerals, and vitamins.

I avoid fried foods. The frying method itself reduces the nutritional value of whatever is in the fryer, and possibly adds dangerous free-radical molecules, which, among other allegations, hasten aging. Frying, of course, will contribute a huge amount of fat to your diet. Instead of frying, I use small amounts of oil in sautés, marinades, and dressings.

The amount of cholesterol in your blood has been linked to cardiovascular disease (simply put, the more there is, the greater the risk), so I've omitted major dietary sources of saturated fat and cholesterol, such as chicken skin, red meat, most cheeses, and egg yolks. Foods from animal sources are not the only culprits; saturated fats from plants, such as hardened vegetable shortenings and palm kernel and coconut oils, can also contribute to an unhealthy heart, even though they don't contain cholesterol, and should be avoided. As with many health issues, factors other than diet also play a role. Your own genetics, whether you are hypertensive, and if you smoke all affect your risk of heart disease.

Protein is consumed in excess in the United States. I recommend limiting portions of lean meats, chicken, and fish to about 3 to 6 ounces per day. Beans, grains, and low-fat dairy products also contain protein, and a combination of these foods provides adequate amounts.

Most of my recipes are made with complex carbohydrates, also called starches. These are grains and beans, corn, peas, and potatoes. Most simple carbohydrates are calorie dense but nutrient deficient because the fiber, vitamins, and minerals are removed during the refining process. I stick with the minimally processed complex carbohydrates, the ones with fiber, flavor, and nutrients intact. White rice, although a complex carbohydrate, has been stripped of much of its germ, oils, vitamins, and fiber. The same differences hold true between whole grain bread and white bread. Processed foods are empty calories, often lacking in flavor. However, there are times when a small amount of white flour makes a better muffin, or when a pasta dish just isn't the same unless it uses white pasta. Within the context of a healthy diet, small amounts of refined foods are quite acceptable.

I rely on generous amounts of fresh vegetables and fruits. Some are high in fiber, most are full of vitamins and minerals, and the majority are comparatively low in calories but robust in flavor. Some fruits and vegetables are known to reduce the risk of cancer. Dark leafy greens, yellow and orange squashes and root vegetables, woodsy mushrooms, and ripe fruits take their rightful place on center stage in my kitchen. These foods are completely satisfying on their own. It is impossible to improve on a sun-ripened, just-picked tomato, on an ear of corn from a local farm, or on a green bean steamed bright and crisp-tender.

I don't count calories because, as long as fat content is low and fiber high, the calories will be low. A gram of fat contains more than twice the calories of a gram of protein or carbohydrates, and besides, not all calories are created equal. Recent research suggests that, of every 100 calories of complex carbohydrate the body takes in, 25 are used up during assimilation and storage, but of 100 calories of fat, only 3 are burned. Some fibrous foods pass right through the body without contributing any calories, which means that simply counting calories does not provide an accurate picture of how many excess calories your body will store as fat; overall dietary composition is more important.

Bodies also burn calories differently. A fit, muscular body burns them more efficiently than a sedentary one—which is one reason why exercise is important to a weight reduction plan.

Although I do believe that too many "bad" foods will make you ill, I cannot accept the notion that specific foods will cure you of your woes. There has never been a single food, acting alone, that can heal the sick.

Oat bran is unlikely to lower cholesterol if it is eaten in a muffin made with butter and eggs. It is the combination of good food and good living that keeps the body healthy. There are no magic, easy solutions, no silver bullets, no shortcuts. All your food choices have an effect.

There are certain ingredients that I have not used in my recipes, but that I do eat occasionally—butter, for one. I'd rather see it and taste it on a slice of bread (and feel decadent) than include it in a recipe (which always needs more than just one pat) that can get along just fine without it.

I never cook with, and rarely eat, some ingredients, such as cream, even though they taste wonderful. They are just too far off course for a low-fat diet. There are no substitutes for these rich products, and imitations fail to satisfy (reduced-fat sour cream tastes "off" to me, and Fettucine Alfredo made with skim milk and cornstarch is a total disaster). But there are so many other ingredients that do make me happy, I don't feel the loss.

My self-imposed dietary guidelines still leave me with an abundance of ingredients. I have a refrigerator full of fruits and vegetables, a cabinet full of spices, jars of beans and grains, a variety of oils, plus raisins, nuts, flours, chicken, fish, milk, cheese, yogurt, and pasta. The limitations I impose are less confining than the average diet of meat and potatoes.

This cookbook is a personal project filled with my opinions and observations. Although I am confident that my recipes will satisfy the nutritional needs of most people, I do encourage you to learn as much as possible about diet and nutrition. Read what you can, listen to your body, and think for yourself.

Stocking the Pantry

Keep your pantry and refrigerator stocked with the basics. Just as an artist can paint new works from the same palette of colors, a cook can create imaginative meals from the same staples. Having all of the basics on hand makes spur-of-the-moment cooking possible. It allows you to prepare a meal even when it looks as though there's nothing in the refrigerator. Besides, even a complicated recipe won't seem forbidding if most of the ingredients are already on your shelves.

Once your shelves are stocked with staples, shopping becomes simple. Each week you only have to buy fresh foods, such as vegetables, fish, chicken, and dairy products. Fresh foods can be bought at local markets as well as at large grocery stores. Getting to know your neighborhood vendors—the local fishmonger or farmer, for example—gives you a sense of community and assures that you obtain the best foodstuffs around.

Light and heat limit shelf life. Don't store foods under or over the stove where it is warm, or in clear glass canisters on the windowsill. Keeping foods in a cool, dark pantry, or in the refrigerator or freezer, helps preserve flavor and nutrients.

Keep the refrigerator cold—below 40 degrees F. Buy and use a glass thermometer to be certain of the temperature. It really does make a difference, especially with your dairy products. And make sure the freezer remains below 0 degrees F. A warmer temperature will permit freezer burn, which means big ice crystals and food spoilage.

Grains and beans look as if they will last forever but are best if used within a year. Over time, their texture and flavor deteriorate.

Pastas and flours will stay fresh for several months. In fact, flours can last almost a year if kept frozen in an airtight container.

Spices that are whole will remain fresh for upwards of 100 years, but ground spices lose their impact within days, and will be dull within months. Dried herbs will be usable from between six months to a year.

All of this may seem picky, but the flavor and texture of food are tied directly to how, and how long, it is stored. The simplest recipes will shine if fresh ingredients are used, and fail if made from ingredients that are past their prime.

Following is a list of what I keep in my pantry, refrigerator, and freezer. It reflects my personal preferences and is meant as a guide only.

Dried Beans, Grains, and Pastas

Beans (navy and pinto)
Lentils (brown and red)
Split peas
Barley
Brown rice
Couscous

Kasha
Spaghetti*
Stubby shaped pasta (such as
   bows, rigatoni, or wheels)*
Udon and soba noodles

Perishables

Carrots
Leeks or scallions
Vegetables in season
Frozen peas and corn
Low-fat cottage cheese

Low-fat yogurt
Lemon juice (Minutemaid comes
   in a squeeze bottle, no additives,
   with a 6-week shelf life when
   defrosted; sold in the freezer case)

---

* 100% whole wheat pasta is a bit too gummy for me, as are some of the poorly made white pastas. In general, the darker the pasta, the heavier it is. I've come across a few brands of whole wheat noodles that I like, but I also use white pasta. It does lack fiber, but I make up for that in the rest of the recipe, and also compensate by eating other whole grains during the day.

Baking and Cooking Needs

Arrowroot powder (a better
thickener than cornstarch)
Baking powder (not low-sodium; it
doesn't taste right or work as well)
Baking soda
Old-fashioned oats
Flour (unbleached white, whole
wheat, and whole wheat pastry)
Raisins
Nuts and seeds (I keep pepitas,
walnuts, and almonds in the freezer)

Tahini
Oil (corn, olive, and sesame)
Frozen apple juice concentrate
Honey
Syrups (malt and maple)
Molasses
Defatted chicken stock
Vinegars (including balsamic,
cider, and red wine)
Sherry
Wine (red and white)

Herbs, Seasonings, and Spices

Basil
Bay leaves
Dill
Marjoram
Oregano
Garlic (fresh)
Ginger (fresh and ground)
Onions (yellow)
Soy sauce
Hot pepper sauce
Seeds (mustard, poppy, and
sesame)
Salt

Peppercorns in a pepper mill
Cayenne pepper
Chili powder
Curry powder
Turmeric
Coriander
Cardamom
Cloves (ground and whole)
Cinnamon (ground and sticks)
Nutmeg (whole) and a nutmeg grater
(there is no comparison between
freshly grated and packaged ground
nutmeg)

Fresh Herbs—How to Keep Them from Going to Waste

Fresh herbs can make a big difference in a recipe; they smell and taste better than dried, although dried are much easier to use. Most of you have probably had the experience of buying a bunch of dill or parsley, using a sprig or two, and putting the rest back into the refrigerator, where it quickly goes limp and then bad. After a few of these frustrating (and expensive) attempts to use fresh herbs, you decide to stick with dried. There are ways to avoid this dilemma.

The most important step in working with fresh herbs is to wash and dry them thoroughly. The best method takes a little extra time but is well worth it. Start by separating the leaves from the stems. (Save the stems for stock or discard them.) Put the leafy parts into a bowl filled with cool water and soak the herbs for a few minutes. Lift them out, discard the water (and the dirt in the bottom), and repeat this step until no sediment collects in the bowl.

After washing them, it is very important to dry the herbs completely. If wet herbs are minced, they turn into mush and deteriorate rapidly. Towels can be used for drying, but they are not effective and can bruise the herbs, shortening their shelf life. Use a salad spinner instead. This inexpensive tool gently removes excess water by centrifugal force.

At this point, the whole leafy parts can be stored in a loosely closed plastic bag in the refrigerator. I've had parsley last this way for two weeks and fresh mint for almost as long. This longevity can be attributed to gentle handling and to starting with the crispest and freshest herbs available.

Many recipes call for minced, or finely chopped herbs. Although the food processor can do this, it tears the leaves too much, limiting the herb's shelf life. A large chef knife is the best tool for mincing herbs, as its smooth blade cuts cleanly. Chop on a large, flat, dry surface, and the task will take little time.

Allow the herbs to dry for about an hour, then put them into covered containers. Minced herbs stay fresh in the refrigerator for a week and sometimes longer, which is certainly longer than if they had remained in the bunch. And herbs that are already minced and ready for the pot are more likely to be used. (Remember, you will need three times more fresh herbs than dried.)

Usually, a bunch of herbs yields more than a cook needs in a week. If this is the case, store the excess in the freezer. Freshly minced herbs will retain their flavor, color, and aroma even after freezing, except for basil which turns black. Keep them in a freezer bag or container and use as needed.

Grains

Generally speaking, grains are the seed-bearing fruits of grasses. They are carbohydrates, commonly called starches. Nutritionists label them "complex carbohydrates" to distinguish them from similar, although simpler, sugars.

Rice, wheat, barley, millet, oats, quinoa, and kasha are in the grain family. If left in their whole form, grains are truly complex because they contain a wealth of nutrients plus fiber. The whole grain contains several layers, from the outer bran and germ, which house most of the vitamins and minerals, to the inner endosperm, which is almost entirely starch and protein.

Whole grains have a lot to recommend them. They are sources of calcium and vitamin B_6, and they are high in fiber. Fiber improves colon health, reduces cancer risk, and helps to prevent diseases such as diverticulitis. Certain fibers, called soluble fiber, can reduce blood cholesterol levels. Barley and oats are good sources of soluble fiber.

White bread, white rice, and white pasta are processed carbohydrates. White bread is often enriched, but, of the two dozen nutrients removed, only about eight are replaced, accompanied by preservatives, flavorings, fillers, and sugars. White rice is little more than starch and protein. In this book I reserve the term complex carbohydrate for those foods that are minimally processed and still retain the wealth of fiber and nutrients they had when harvested.

Buying whole grains in a natural food store can be a confusing experience. In addition to rows of bulk foods, which, among other items, may include six types of brown rice, there are boxes and bags of other unfamiliar grains. There are a lot of similarities among grains, however, and the same basic cooking technique applies to all of them.

When buying any whole grain, look for kernels that are not broken and that are free from dust (broken grains cook into a sticky mass). Green kernels were picked while immature and should also be avoided.

Grains contain natural oils and will go rancid if not handled properly. This is one reason why grains often are processed and degerminated—to prolong shelf life. Make sure that what you purchase is fresh. Buy from a store that has a high turnover of goods, or that refrigerates its stock. Buy only as much as you need for a few months, or keep grains in the freezer, where they will last a year.

Cooking grains is a very simple process. In most cases, they should be cooked in double their volume of water. (See chart for exceptions.) First, bring the water to a boil. Once the water is boiling, rinse the grain under cool water to rid it of dust, then pour it right into the pot. Immersion in hot water seals the starch onto the kernel and prevents stickiness. If the grain is rinsed too far ahead of time, starch will be released into the cooking water, and the end product will be mushy.

Reduce the boil to a simmer, cover the pot, and cook until all of the water is absorbed. It is not necessary to stir during cooking, but it's okay if you do. If you like grains soft, add an extra quarter cup of water to the simmering pot. If you like them fluffy, stir with a fork after they're done, and let them sit, covered, in the pot but off the burner for 10 minutes before serving. This extra steaming time improves the texture of all cooked grains.

You can be as creative as you like when cooking grains. Combine different kinds, such as wheat berries and short-grain brown rice. Use stock or tomato juice instead of water. Add herbs and vegetables. The ways to prepare them are endless.

Grain Cooking Chart

Unless otherwise noted, the proportion of water to grain is 2 to 1.

GRAIN	TEXTURE/ FLAVOR/USES	SPECIAL COOKING INSTRUCTIONS
Long-grain brown rice	Use in pilafs	40 minutes cooking time
Short-grain brown rice	Nutty flavor	40 minutes cooking time

GRAIN	TEXTURE/ FLAVOR/USES	SPECIAL COOKING INSTRUCTIONS
Sweet rice	Sticky; sweet; use in puddings	Cook with extra water
Wild rice	Earthy flavor	50 minutes cooking time
Brown basmati	Aromatic Indian rice, smells like popcorn when cooked	40 minutes cooking time
Barley	Chewy, mild flavor; use in soups and salads	3 parts water to 1 part grain; 1½ hours cooking time
Buckwheat (also called kasha)	Assertive, unique flavor	15 minutes cooking time for whole kernel; 10 minutes for cracked
Bulgur wheat (also called cracked wheat)	Mild flavor; use in salads, pilafs	15 minutes cooking time for coarsely ground; finely ground just needs soaking
Wheat berries	Chewy, sweet, nutty	2½ parts water to 1 part grain; 1½ hours cooking time
Couscous	Slightly processed grain made from wheat; mild flavor, soft texture; use in salads, stuffings, with sauces	Put in boiling water, cover, turn off burner; let sit until all water is absorbed: 10-15 minutes
Millet	Light, mild flavor	3 parts water to 1 part grain; 20-35 minutes cooking time
Quinoa	Delicate flavor (see page 44 for details)	Wash well, dry toast, then simmer; 15 minutes cooking time; expands to about 4 times its un- cooked size

Beans

Most of you have a jar or two of beans on a shelf in your kitchen that has been there for ages. Perhaps once a year you attempt a bean dish, with indifferent success, and then put the unused beans back on the shelf. This is unfortunate because beans, like oatmeal, are one of the comfort foods. They fill you up, nourish you, and leave you feeling good.

Beans are an inexpensive, fat-free source of protein, vitamins, and minerals, and complex carbohydrates, providing quantities of soluble fiber.

Dried beans are in the legume family. They are grown in a shell or pod, harvested when mature, shucked, and dried. Purchased in a hard, inedible state, they require several steps of preparation before being eaten. First, they are soaked in water to soften and expand them. Next, they are cooked in more liquid, sometimes for hours, then seasoned in yet another step. This does take time, but does not require close attention or special skills. Because cooked beans freeze well, those several hours spent in the kitchen can be a source of meals for months to come. And some legumes, notably lentils and split peas, do not require as much preparation. These will be ready, start to finish, in less than an hour.

Dried beans look as though they will last forever, but they don't. Stored in glass jars, away from heat and sunlight, beans will stay fresh for nine months to a year. The longer they are stored, the longer they take to cook. Old beans, even after hours of simmering, have a tough, mealy texture and unappealing flavor. No wonder a person who tries a bean recipe once a year, using the same old beans that have been beautifying the kitchen windowsill, is less than enthusiastic about cooking legumes.

Age is not the only thing that affects bean flavor. Beans vary in quality. I've found that organically grown beans sold in natural food stores are fresher, brighter in color, cook faster, and taste far better than the beans in plastic bags at supermarkets. Whether this results from how they were grown, the seed variety, or the way they were packaged and stored, I do not know.

Beans are often sold in bulk. As a rule of thumb, 1 cup of dried beans weighs about half a pound and yields about 3 cups of cooked.

Before cooking, sort through the beans, then wash them well. The machines that do the harvesting sometimes cannot tell the difference between a bean and a pebble, so it behooves you to be observant. Beans cannot be washed thoroughly before packaging because moisture causes spoilage; therefore, they must be cleansed of soil and dust. Wash only the amount that you are about to use.

Most beans need to be soaked for at least 4 hours to cut the cooking time by half. This step can be done conveniently overnight, or in the morning before leaving for work. Because the beans will swell to nearly twice their original size, place them in water that is three times their dry volume. Any beans that float should be discarded.

An alternative to the long soak is to put the beans and water into a pot, bring to a rolling boil for 2 minutes, then cover, turn off the heat, and let sit for 1 hour. If all this soaking seems like too much effort, don't give up on beans. Lentils and split peas do not need to be soaked at all.

Although the soaking water contains nutrients that leaked from the beans, I discard it because it usually has some silt. Also, beans will cause less flatulence if they are cooked in fresh water. (This is true: It is the bacteria that live inside your body that cause gas. They "eat" certain carbohydrates from the beans, but by throwing out the soaking water, they don't have as much to feed on. If gas deters you from eating beans, you might discard and replace the cooking liquid several times as the beans simmer, for again, this gives the bacteria less of what they eat.)

After soaking, beans take 1 to 2 hours to cook. Place them over a moderate flame in plenty of water in a large, heavy pot. (Cast iron is a good choice because it retains heat, contributes iron to food, and cooks the beans evenly and slowly.) Skim off the foam that rises to the surface, cover the pot, and stir occasionally to keep the beans from sticking to the bottom. When a bean can be mashed between two fingers, and is soft throughout (not dry or crumbly), the beans are done.

Salt and acidic ingredients extend the cooking time, so it is best not to add them until the beans are about done.

Beans come in a great variety of colors, shapes, and sizes. In general, the smaller, whiter beans are milder and take less time to cook. These are often used in pâtés and soups. The mottled or solid brown beans, such as kidney and pinto, are used for stews and chilies, and the darkest, purple-black beans are more assertively flavored and work well in soups

Hot Pepper Sauce

Tabasco, made from hot, red, ripe peppers grown on an island in Louisiana, is just one brand of hot sauce. There are plenty of other hot sauces on the market which have loyal, if not fanatical, devotees. Generally reddish in hue, hot pepper sauce consists, basically, of chili peppers, vinegar, salt, and occasionally other spices. When a recipe calls for this ingredient, use your favorite brand.

Chinese hot sauces are different. These jars of bean paste or chili sauce can cause an inferno on your tongue. If you can taste beyond the burning sensation, you will detect a difference in flavor between an oriental hot sauce and one from the deep South.

Hot sauce is also the name of a condiment that can be used as ketchup is. It goes well with bean enchiladas or grilled chicken, and is commercially available or can be made from scratch (see page 186).

and casseroles. Orange and greenish-brown lentils are sweet and go nicely in curries and soups.

In spite of their differences, just about any bean or legume can be substituted for another. All blend well with seasonings and other additions. You can, of course, purchase beans that are already cooked. Those that come in glass jars often have better flavor. Avoid the canned ones packed with lard or other fats. Some have citric acid added, which is not harmful. Most are overly salty. If you do use canned beans, rinse them to remove the metallic taste. The texture and flavor are inferior to that of freshly cooked dried, but they are a convenience, and a canned bean is better than no bean at all.

The Onion Family

The reasons why members of the onion family (which includes chives, garlic, leeks, and shallots) impart the flavors and aromas (and tears to the eyes) that they do could fill a textbook. Oils, sugars, and aromatic circular molecules are released into the air when they are cut. Each member of this diverse family of plants contributes something unique to a recipe. Following is a short description of what each has to offer.

Garlic—Garlic is merchandised in four forms in the market. Fresh garlic is sold either in small boxes or loose. Because packaged garlic usually has tiny cloves, which are annoying to peel, I avoid it. Buy the loose garlic, which you can inspect for size and freshness. Garlic should be firm, with paperlike skin, and free from mold and green shoots. Store along with onions in a cool, dark place, but not in the refrigerator, where moisture will hasten its deterioration.

Garlic is also sold minced, mixed with oil, and packed in jars. It is handy to use in this form, but has an unpleasant aroma and slightly bitter aftertaste when cooked. You can prepare an equally convenient but better-tasting product at home. Mince 1 or 2 bulbs of garlic (easily done in a food processor fitted with metal blade), and store in a glass jar in the refrigerator. Without oil, it will stay fresh for almost two weeks; with oil, it will last for months.

I also put whole, crushed cloves of garlic into my favorite oil. The garlic can be used or discarded after a week or two. The oil (stored in the refrigerator) imparts a mild garlic taste to foods without the texture or assertiveness of the garlic itself.

Dried and powdered garlic is not a substitute for fresh. It lacks the complexity, the aroma, and the subtle sweetness of fresh garlic and leaves a bitter aftertaste. There are a few recipes, however, in which it is useful. It mixes well in breadings and dressings, in which bits of fresh garlic might be too intense. Also, because the flavor of fresh garlic gets stronger over time, try dry garlic in salad dressings that are meant to last for at least a week, for a quieter, more consistent garlic flavor.

Leeks—Leeks have a milder flavor than other onions, and are often used in soups and Chinese stir-fries. They provide an alternative flavor when the traditional cooking onion would be overbearing or has been overused in a meal.

Leeks must be washed thoroughly, because the soil that is piled around the base of the leek as it grows gets into every layer. To remove the dirt, cut off the bottom (root end) of the leek, slit the stem halfway through to expose all of the layers, and rinse well under running water.

Many recipes call for the white section of the leek only because it is the most tender and flavorful part. If some of the green leaves are fresh and are not tough or mushy, they, too, can be included.

Scallions—A scallion, also called a green onion, is the immature stage of a variety of onions. It has a white or sometimes light purple bulb and dark green shoots. Especially suited to salads and chilled soups, it is mild in flavor and good either cooked or uncooked.

Choose scallions with small, firm bulbs. This part contains the strongest flavor. If the tops are fresh, they, too, can be included; their green color is usually a welcome addition.

Shallots—A shallot is a garlic-shaped bulb which has a purple, onionlike clove when the skin is peeled away. Most supermarkets sell shallots and often stock them next to the garlic, packaged in boxes similar to those in which garlic is sold. Fresh shallots are firm and free from mold and green shoots. They can be stored with onions in a cool, dark place. The flavor of shallots is more subtle and elegant than that of its cousins. They are used in a variety of ways, including French sauces, salad dressings, and Thai dishes.

Types of Onions—Onions are included in so many dishes that they can appear at every meal, from breakfast to lunch to dinner, and for each of these, the type of onion used can, and often should, be different. Each varies from the next, and the proper onion choice can make or break a recipe.

The **Spanish** onion is a large, yellow bulb, usually sold loose and by the pound in the market. It is sweet but needs cooking before use. Because of its large size, it is convenient to use when a lot of chopped onion is needed, for only a couple have to be peeled. I once got 8 cups of chopped onion from 1 big Spanish bulb. For this reason, they are the onion of choice for many restaurants.

The **yellow onion** is a smaller version of the Spanish. It has a more assertive flavor and is preferable in soups and stews, because the long cooking times would cause much of the Spanish onion flavor to disappear.

The **red onion** is actually purple in color. It is sweet and mild, and used raw in salads or in summer soups, such as gazpacho.

Pearl onions are small white bulbs that are mild and slightly sweet. They are perfect for stews or as a side dish.

There are other, more exotic onions to be found, but they generally are not as readily available as those just discussed. The **vidalia**, for instance, is one of the best known of the finer-tasting onions. It is so sweet that some onion aficionados eat it raw, like an apple. Grown in Georgia, it is available only late in the spring. The **wala-wala** from Washington has its own following, and the **Bermuda** onion, a large, round, whitish bulb, makes perfect onion rings. It also is often cut into thick slices and served on top of toasted bagels.

Salt

There is no doubt that salt is consumed in excess in this country. With one small meal at a fast-food restaurant providing more than the body's daily requirement, it is no wonder that salt is a contributing factor to the poor health of many. And since the link between sodium and hypertension has been well publicized, there is a need for recipes that are low in salt. The matter is much more complicated, however, than simply limiting salt consumption.

Sodium is only one of a multitude of minerals needed by the body. Calcium, magnesium, and potassium are also necessary for the body's smooth functioning, especially when it comes to the regulation of blood pressure. Some scientists believe that these other minerals (or their lack) are as important in regulating blood pressure as sodium is.

Eliminating salt will have an effect, to be sure, but the extent will vary due to many factors. Genetically, some individuals are more susceptible to salt's ability to raise blood pressure than are others. On the flip side, there are those who are entirely unresponsive to the amount of salt in their diets, and show no change in blood pressure even when salt consumption is eliminated altogether. Increasing age affects how the body reacts to salt, and overall diet is also a big factor. Eliminating salt from a high-fat, low-fiber diet will do little good, especially for a sedentary and overweight individual.

For the average person, it appears that too much salt is harmful but its total elimination is unnecessary. What this suggests is that you should be sensible but not fanatical about salt. It is generally recommended that total sodium intake be limited to less than 3 grams per day. (There are about 2 grams of sodium in 1 teaspoon of table salt.) This does allow for some salt in cooking, but not for a heavy hand with the salt shaker at the dinner table, or for salty snacks, or for frequenting fast-food establishments. Condiments and seasonings that taste salty should not be part of the daily fare, and care should be taken in choosing all packaged foods, from crackers to salad dressings.

For a cook, it is a relief to know that some salt can be used in recipes. Sodium does much more than just add the flavor of salt to food. Chemically, it changes the molecules that stimulate the taste buds. Without salt, those very same molecules are not as capable of exciting the taste buds, and the food seems bland. Obtaining this reaction does not require large quantities of salt; sometimes so little is needed that the flavor of the salt itself cannot be detected. There is no rule for how much salt to use; it differs from recipe to recipe, and is learned through trial and error.

Soy Sauce

The underlying seasoning for many Asian dishes is soy sauce. This dark liquid has been a cornerstone of Chinese cuisine since the second century B.C. From China, it traveled to Japan, Malaysia, and other Eastern countries. In more recent times, it has gained a strong foothold here in the United States.

There is some confusion as to exactly what soy sauce is. This is understandable since there are several types and the names are not always consistent with what is in the bottle. A true soy sauce, called shoyu in Japan, is made from only four ingredients: water, wheat, soybeans, and salt. It is aged for at least a year, during which time the liquid ferments, and the characteristic salty, pungent flavor forms. Tamari is not the same thing as soy sauce. It is a close cousin and is made in a similar fashion, but without the wheat. It is saltier and more intense than soy sauce, and is traditionally used only as a condiment.

There are big differences among brands of soy sauce also. Chinese soy sauce is stronger than Japanese. Dark soy sauce contains molasses, and is used for specific recipes such as twice-cooked pork. Light soy sauce is the regular Chinese soy; it is not low in sodium. Because many Americans prefer a milder soy sauce, Kikkoman, a Japanese brand, is widely used in the United States, even in Chinese restaurants.

The best soy sauces are costly because they are made in the time-honored, slow tradition of the Orient. Food technologists have invented a less expensive, faster way to make a similar product, although I hesitate to call it soy sauce. It uses soybean extracts, and a chemical process instead of fermentation. Everything about the cheaper fake soy sauces is inferior. Some have caramel color and sugars added. All are missing the complex undertones of a naturally brewed soy sauce. Their predominant flavor comes from salt.

Soy sauce is made with salt and it is salty; it is not a salt substitute. A teaspoon of salt contains four to five times more sodium than does a teaspoon of soy sauce. Since soy sauce is a strongly flavored condiment, it can be used in smaller quantities than salt, resulting in a recipe with less sodium. Low-sodium soy sauces are available, and I've tried them, but their flavors are so weak that I have to use twice as much to get the full impact of regular soy sauce.

Because soy sauce is a natural flavor enhancer, I use it in other dishes besides Asian. It works well in chili and bean dishes, and is equally welcome in all manner of soups.

Miso

Miso is a fermented product, similar to soy sauce in that it contains soybeans, salt, and a culture. But miso is a paste, not a liquid, and some misos are made from grains and beans other than soy. Each type of miso varies by color and flavor; some differences are pronounced, while some are subtle.

As a rule, the darker misos, such as those made from black or red beans, are more intense in flavor that the white and yellow misos. All contain salt but the darker misos taste saltier. Generally, a half teaspoon of table salt is equivalent to a tablespoon of miso.

A versatile ingredient, miso can be used as bouillon, as a seasoning, or as the base for a marinade. It is sold in large-sized quantities at natural food stores. Because a little goes a long way, the purchase may seem excessive, but miso lasts for years in the refrigerator, so it doesn't hurt to keep it around.

Sweeteners

When babies are given their first taste of something sweet, they express their delight with a smile. It is an innate reaction, which we continue to exhibit the rest of our lives. Sweet foods give us pleasure. America's sweet tooth, however, has gotten out of hand. The average person consumes more than 100 pounds of sugar and other sweeteners in a year. This amounts to about 25% of an individual's yearly caloric intake.

Despite its popularity, sugar receives and has earned a lot of negative press. It causes dental cavities; as a source of empty calories, it contributes to the alarming amount of obesity in this country; and it is linked to heart disease, high blood pressure, and diabetes. Studies have shown that, for certain groups within the population, sugar has a detrimental effect on mental health, mood, and children's learning abilities.

These studies have documented what happens when large amounts of sugar are consumed. When sugar is consumed in moderation, its effect on many of these diseases and their symptoms is negligible, but the question remains, what is a moderate amount? The answer depends on each individual.

I use sugars and make desserts, but justify this by fitting sweets into a nutritious and fiber-filled diet. I seldom eat packaged, processed desserts, which are often made from inferior ingredients and laced with chemicals, and are so sweet that they are not particularly appetizing. But I do enjoy a big piece of homemade apple pie, or oatmeal cookies. And I glaze chicken with orange marmalade and add raisins to brown rice.

There is continuing controversy as to whether natural sugars are less harmful than white sugar. Part of this answer can be found by looking at the chemical structure of sugars, and how the body reacts to them. All sugars are simple carbohydrates that are absorbed rapidly by the intestinal tract. The rate of absorption affects the amount of sugar being carried by the blood. The body likes to keep the blood sugar level constant; if the level gets too high or too low, it can be a cause for concern. If ingested without other foods, all sugars, natural or otherwise, are rapidly assimilated by the body. If much sugar is consumed, the system overloads. Fat and fiber slow down the absorption of sugars, and, in fact, are more important for maintaining healthy blood sugar levels than are the alternative sugars, such as honey or maple syrup.

Fruits are naturally sweet and high in sugars. In their whole form, they supply a fiber called pectin, plus plenty of vitamins and minerals. As juice, they don't contribute fiber, but do contain some vitamins that are healthful. Bottled fructose is the simple sugar that is extracted from fruit. It supposedly does not affect blood sugar levels, but it does have other problems. It raises the level of triglycerides (a type of fat) in the blood, which can be a serious health risk.

Some of my recipes call for frozen fruit juice concentrate, which is sold in the freezer section of any market. This is mainly comprised of simple sugars, mostly fructose, and is at least twice as concentrated as fresh or bottled juice. Some stores sell concentrated fruit juice in bottles; this is even more concentrated than the frozen (and much more expensive). Used in excess, concentrated fruit juice will make a recipe taste like cooked fruit juice, but used in moderation it adds a delicate, fruity dimension to a recipe. Defrosted, the concentrate will last in the refrigerator for about ten days. I keep it in the freezer and use it as needed.

Malt syrups are another type of sweetener that some claim does not affect blood sugar levels. Malt syrups are made from either barley, corn, or rice. An enzyme is placed into a slurry made from the grain, which breaks the complex carbohydrates down into simple sugars. Because the enzyme doesn't completely break down the starch, the malt syrup is less sweet than other sweeteners and slightly more complex. Malt syrups have a unique flavor well suited to many recipes. There are several brands for sale, all of which have different tastes. I've found that the lighter colored ones are the sweetest and lightest in flavor. Keep opened jars in the refrigerator.

Honey and maple syrup are two of the sweetest of the sweeteners, and are rapidly absorbed by the intestinal tract. There is no evidence that they are any easier on blood sugar levels than white sugar. And although they do contain trace amounts of minerals and vitamins, they have minimal nutritional value.

Molasses is one of the few sugars with noticeable quantities of nutrients. Unfortunately, because of its strong, distinctive flavor, it is only useful in a few recipes. Blackstrap molasses is loaded with vitamins and minerals, but its flavor is so intense that I don't cook with it at all.

Maple sugar and date sugar are very expensive dry sweeteners. To make date sugar, the dates are dried and then ground. No figures are available, but it is likely that some nutrients remain after this processing.

Maple sugar is dehydrated maple syrup. Sucanat is the trade name of dried sugar cane juice. It is not the same as brown sugar, because it is not highly processed and it retains much of the cane's nutritive value. All of these dried sweeteners are alternatives to white sugar, and with their unique flavors, they contribute more than just sweetness to a recipe.

Raw or turbinado sugar is simply white sugar that has not been bleached. It is almost identical to table sugar, except that it still has some impurities in it. Brown sugar is colored white sugar. Corn syrup is a liquid sweetener that is as refined and processed as white sugar.

And what of white sugar? Its effect on blood sugar levels is about the same as any other sweetener, and none of them provides much in the way of nutritive value. But white sugar does remarkable things for baked goods. It adds a pure, sweet taste that allows other flavors to shine through. It retains moisture and freshness, and is necessary for making light batters. I don't cook with white sugar, however, and try to avoid it when I eat out. This is a personal choice, and I will share my reasoning with you.

White sugar and other highly refined sweeteners, such as corn syrup and fructose, have no flavor and only contribute sweetness. They can be slipped into almost anything unnoticed, and food manufacturers use them in everything from soups to peanut butter to salad dressings to french fries. I avoid commercial products that contain refined sugars, and have learned to dislike the ubiquitous sweetness found in many prepared foods. At home, I use alternative sweeteners because their flavors limit the amount that I can add to a recipe, making them self-regulating. Extra white sugar can be added to a pie with little harm, but extra honey would ruin it.

White sugar is a highly processed, chemically refined substance. It may contain traces of substances from the manufacturing process that I do not want to eat. Also of concern is that as a crop, it has been a major factor in the deterioration of the economies of many Third World countries, lessening the ability of these countries to be self-sufficient, and has destroyed the land so that it is unsuitable for other uses. I don't want to be a part of that.

One final, opinionated word. Artificial sweeteners like NutraSweet are not acceptable sugar substitutes. The jury is still out as to whether they are health risks, but I retain my skepticism about them. The idea of a guilt-free, calorie-free sweetener is appealing, but the truth is that it is not effective in weight reduction. Since the introduction of artificial sweeteners, consumption of processed white sugars and corn syrup in the United States has gone up, not down. Obesity has not decreased. These sweeteners have only increased our craving for more sugar, which is obviously not the answer to the problem.

Oils

Although many recipes specify a generic vegetable oil, more and more cooks are selecting specific oils to suit individual recipes. There is a wide spectrum of oils from which to choose, each with its own unique flavor, cooking characteristics, and fatty acid composition.

All oils have several things in common. They are made from plants and are extracted from seeds or nuts. Oils are liquid at room temperature, can be heated to high temperatures (water can only get up to 212 degrees F, but some oils can reach 400 degrees F before smoking), and do not contain cholesterol (cholesterol is derived from animal sources and, as mentioned, all oils come from plants).

Oils are categorized by how they have been processed. Unrefined oils have been minimally processed and made without preservatives. Because they turn rancid when exposed to heat and light, they need to be refrigerated after opening. All oils are heated, but the unrefined ones are heated at lower temperatures; therefore, they retain nutrients that are lost to the more refined oils.

Highly processed oils are chemically extracted (not pressed), refined, bleached, deodorized, strained, and treated to remove cloudiness. No wonder so many oils taste the same!

Some oils are hydrogenated, which means they are made saturated through a chemical process. Oils are hydrogenated in order to convert the liquid into a solid, extend the shelf life, and raise the smoke point (a necessity for fast-food fryers).

A potential health risk associated with oils comes from the formation of free radicals. These are unstable molecules that occur when an oil becomes rancid or when the fat is exposed to high heat—for example, during frying or processing. These free radicals may play a role in aging and are also believed to destroy biological tissues. By refrigerating opened bottles of oil and by avoiding fried foods, the risk of damage from free radicals can be lessened.

I limit the type and quantity of oil in the kitchen, but I continue to use it because flavors are fat soluble. This means that, without some fat to hold onto, the flavors disappear, which is why fat-free recipes often taste bland, even when herbs have been doubled. Fat blends and mellows ingredients so that seasonings work together without being too sharp. Fat imparts some flavor of its own, which, depending on the oil, can be quite noticeable.

Oil is used in bread baking to promote elasticity and in baked goods for moisture and texture. Oil heats to a higher temperature than other liquids, such as stock and wine, and because it can penetrate foods more quickly and deeply, it is the perfect choice for stir-fries. The high temperature that fats reach is necessary for browning and crisping foods. When foods brown, new flavors are created that cannot be duplicated at the lower temperatures used for steaming or sautéing in fat-free stock. For example, onions cooked in oil caramelize and sweeten. Onions cooked in water in a nonstick pan just become soft. The two effects are worlds apart.

It is not necessary, however, to use excessive quantities of oil to achieve the benefits of fat. A tablespoon or less is often enough, although each recipe is different. Try starting your sauté with a teaspoon of oil, then switching to stock, wine, or juice after the oil is absorbed. Because these liquids will evaporate faster than oil, add small amounts as needed during the course of cooking. Also, because liquids other than oil do not get as hot, it will take longer to cook foods in them.

Occasionally, you can eliminate the oil from a recipe altogether. It takes trial and error, but you will get a feel for it. Some of the recipes in this book are fat-free; those with oil use as little as possible to get the best results.

Types of Oils and Their Uses

The saturation, flavor, and smoke point (how hot an oil can get before smoking) are determined by the plant from which the oil was extracted. Oil blends or highly processed oils tend to have neutral flavors. I prefer to use oils that retain the distinctiveness of their origins, making each teaspoon of oil an important contribution to the recipe.

Canola (also called rapeseed)—lowest in saturated fat of all the oils. This mild oil is monounsaturated and useful when olive oil is too strong in flavor.

Corn—a good all-purpose oil. Deep yellow in color, and slightly richer tasting than the other polyunsaturates, it foams when heated, so its uses for sauté are limited.

Cottonseed—not grown under the laws that govern food crops; it has a high level of chemical and pesticide residues and should be avoided.

Nut—wonderful, rich flavors. They are best for salad dressings or added to sauces. They break down under high heat and are expensive.

Olive—fruity flavor and prominent aroma. Virgin or extra-virgin has the most robust character and is full of nutritive value. Olive oil labeled "pure" is one of the last extractions from the olive and is far from pure. It has been blended, had its acid level balanced, and sometimes is deodorized. Like wine, olive oil is affected by soil, weather, and harvesting techniques. Each brand tastes different. Some extra-virgin is too fruity for anything but salad dressings. Generally, the darker the color, the stronger the flavor. Olive oils stay fresh in the pantry for a few months, but should be kept refrigerated for longer periods. As do all monounsaturates, olive oil clouds and thickens in the refrigerator, but clears when brought to room temperature.

Peanut—another monounsaturate. A flavorful oil often used for stir-frying.

Safflower—a stronger-flavored oil good for sautés and salads.

Sesame—a distinctive, assertive oil used to add flavor. It smokes if subjected to high heat. Toasted sesame oil has even more character and is used as a seasoning.

Soy and Sunflower—light, all-purpose vegetable oils.

SALADS
AND DRESSINGS

A tossed salad used to consist of iceberg lettuce and a tomato wedge. Although still commonly served, this is not the template. Today's salads are more creative, and they go far beyond a bowl of lettuce. A salad can be mixed greens served as the first course, marinated vegetables, or a serving of cucumbers and yogurt. Increasingly, salads are becoming the main event.

Chicken salads. Pasta salads. The basis of many a gourmet store's business is the take-out luncheon salad. Even fast-food chains have embraced the idea of serving salad as a meal. Unfortunately, these packaged versions are often high in fat and low in food value and freshness. Salads made at home, on the other hand, can be everything you wish—convenient, healthful, interesting, and flavorful.

What do you dress these salads with? The classic homemade vinaigrette has two times as much oil as vinegar. The typical store-bought variety contains excessive calories, saturated fats, preservatives, chemicals, and salt (though there are exceptions). Dressings with a sour cream or mayonnaise base are so high in fat and cholesterol that they do not have a place in this book. And commercial substitutes for these products leave a bad taste in the mouth.

Dressings are necessary. They moisten and flavor salads and in some cases preserve them. In the following recipes I use oils and salt sparingly, but the results are satisfying and appealing. The most basic dressing of oil, vinegar, and freshly cracked pepper graces a salad just as appetizingly as does a more complex concoction. There are some tricks involved, such as including a dash of red wine, combining lemon juice and vinegar, incorporating a judicious amount of mustard, and using only the best oil.

Fresh garlic is fine for salads eaten the day they are made, but after a few days the garlic flavor becomes overpowering. Also, some of you may object to eating raw garlic, no matter how finely it is minced. For these reasons, I often substitute garlic powder—a quarter teaspoon replaces a small clove of fresh garlic

Vinaigrettes perfectly fit my cooking style and my kitchen. I simply put the ingredients into a glass jar, cover, and shake. Most will keep for a couple of weeks in the refrigerator. A good vinaigrette should have a balance of flavors with herbs and seasonings adding interest but not conflict.

SALADS AND DRESSINGS

Red Wine Vinaigrette

Red wine softens the sharpness of vinegar and lends a richness to this dressing.

1 tablespoon	lemon juice
1 tablespoon	red wine vinegar
1 tablespoon	red wine
2 tablespoons	olive oil
1 teaspoon	water
¼ teaspoon	salt
⅛ teaspoon	freshly ground pepper
½ teaspoon	dry mustard
½ teaspoon	dijon mustard
1 teaspoon	dried basil
1	small clove garlic, finely minced
1	slice of onion, minced, or ¼ teaspoon onion powder

Whisk all ingredients together in a bowl, or combine in a glass jar, cover, and shake well.

Yields ½ cup, 8 1-tablespoon servings

33 CALORIES PER TABLESPOON: 0 G PROTEIN, 3 G FAT, 1 G CARBOHYDRATE; 71 MG SODIUM; 0 MG CHOLESTEROL

Balsamic Vinaigrette

Complex, intense flavors in an easy-to-prepare dressing.

¼ cup	olive oil
3 tablespoons	balsamic vinegar
1 tablespoon	lemon juice
1⁄16 teaspoon	salt
⅛ teaspoon	freshly ground pepper

Combine ingredients in a glass jar, cover, and shake well.

Yields ½ cup, 8 1-tablespoon servings

61 CALORIES PER TABLESPOON: 0 G PROTEIN, 7 G FAT, 1 G CARBOHYDRATE; 16 MG SODIUM; 0 MG CHOLESTEROL

Tomato Vinaigrette

Tomato juice mellows the vinegar and reduces the amount of oil needed.

1 cup	red wine vinegar
¼ cup	olive oil
¼ cup	frozen apple juice concentrate
1½ cups	tomato juice
1	small clove garlic, minced, or
	¼ teaspoon garlic powder
1 teaspoon	onion powder
1 tablespoon	dijon mustard
1 teaspoon	dried oregano
½ teaspoon	dried tarragon
dash	cayenne pepper

Whisk all ingredients together in a small bowl until blended, or combine in a glass jar, cover, and shake well.

Yields 3 cups, 48 1-tablespoon servings

15 CALORIES PER TABLESPOON: 0 G PROTEIN, 1 G FAT, 1 G CARBOHYDRATE; 32 MG SODIUM; 0 MG CHOLESTEROL

Mustard Vinaigrette

Mustard is a natural emulsifier, which means that it holds other ingredients together—in suspension. When you shake this dressing, it will stay mixed longer than the others.

¼ cup	olive oil
¼ cup	red wine vinegar
1 teaspoon	prepared mustard
¼ teaspoon	soy sauce
1 teaspoon	lemon juice
	freshly ground pepper to taste

Combine ingredients in a glass jar, cover, and shake well.

Yields just over ½ cup, 8 1-tablespoon servings

61 CALORIES PER TABLESPOON: 0 G PROTEIN, 7 G FAT, 1 G CARBOHYDRATE; 19 MG SODIUM; 0 MG CHOLESTEROL

Perfect Tossed Salad

Tossed salads should be fresh, refreshing, beautiful and inviting, vivid in color and clear in flavor. To accomplish this, each ingredient must be handled and selected with care. A perfect tossed salad is not hard to make, but it does require attention to detail.

The first and most important rule is that all ingredients must be fresh. Lettuce is the base of most salads, and its texture is crucial. Buy crisp lettuce and discard crumpled, outer leaves. Store in the vegetable bin of your refrigerator, where it will stay fresher.

Greens must always be washed well, and this should be done carefully to preserve crispness. Rinse the whole leaves in cool water. Soak in water only if the lettuce is very gritty or muddy. After washing, tear the leaves into pieces that fit easily on a fork, handling each leaf gently. Do not twist. Crease marks quickly turn into brown, mushy lines.

Next, dry the lettuce in a salad spinner, and store in a loosely closed bag. Because lettuce prepared in this way will stay fresh for several days, one session in the kitchen will yield enough salad for a week. A fresh bowl of greens, ready to eat, almost never goes to waste, whereas a wilting head of lettuce usually ends up in the trash.

A perfect tossed salad does not have to be complicated. It can be composed simply of fresh greens—iceberg lettuce alone or a combination of varieties, such as Romaine, green leaf, and Boston. The more exotic arugula, dandelion leaves, and radicchio add a dramatic touch and sharper flavor to a salad, but use them in moderation as they can be overwhelming.

Other vegetables tossed in with the leafy greens must also be fresh and handled carefully. Trim bell peppers of their white membranes, slice mushrooms thinly, and grate the carrots.

Some vegetables fade well before the lettuce does: mushrooms turn soggy and brown, bell peppers get slimy, and cucumbers exude water when left in a tossed salad. Therefore, add these just before serving. Cabbage, carrots, and snowpeas stay fresh longer and can be tossed in early. Because dressings will wilt lettuce, they, too, should be used just prior to the meal.

If the salad makings are fresh and carefully handled, the salad will be wonderful. If you compose it with attention to color, texture, and balanced flavors, it will be perfect.

Two Mustard Dressing

A thick, creamy, low-fat dressing with just the right balance of flavors.

2 cups	buttermilk
2 tablespoons	dijon mustard
3 tablespoons	pommery mustard
1 tablespoon	frozen apple juice concentrate

Combine ingredients in a glass jar, cover, and shake well.

Yields 2¼ cups, 36 1-tablespoon servings

8 CALORIES PER TABLESPOON: 1 G PROTEIN, 0 G FAT, 1 G CARBOHYDRATE; 42 MG SODIUM; 1 MG CHOLESTEROL

Dressed Asparagus

This dressing has character, but does not mask the asparagus flavor.

1 pound	asparagus, trimmed
1 slice	ginger (about the size of a quarter)
1½ teaspoons	vinegar (preferably rice vinegar, found in Asian, gourmet, and natural food stores)
¼ teaspoon	honey
1 teaspoon	sesame oil (or toasted sesame oil, which has a stronger flavor)
1½ teaspoons	soy sauce
4 drops	hot pepper sauce

1. Steam the asparagus until it is cooked but still has "snap," sometimes referred to as crisp-tender.
2. Meanwhile, combine the remaining ingredients, and mix well.
3. While the asparagus is still hot, toss it with the dressing.
4. Discard the ginger before serving. Serve warm or chilled.

Serves 4

57 CALORIES PER SERVING: 5 G PROTEIN, 2 G FAT, 9 G CARBOHYDRATE; 136 MG SODIUM; 0 MG CHOLESTEROL

Carrot and Mint Salad

A colorful mixture with great eye appeal, this salad travels well and is ideal for picnics.

3 slices	red onion, minced (about 1½ tablespoons)
1 tablespoon	cider vinegar
3 tablespoons	water
1½ tablespoons	minced fresh mint
⅛ teaspoon	salt
1 teaspoon	lemon juice
½ pound	carrots, grated on largest hole
1 teaspoon	corn oil

1. Combine the onion, vinegar, 1 tablespoon of the water, mint, salt, and lemon juice, blending well.
2. Sauté the carrots in the oil and remaining 2 tablespoons water until they just start to soften. Toss the dressing in with the hot carrots and serve immediately or chill.

Time saver: Using a food processor fitted with grater, grate the carrots, remove them from the processor bowl, and replace the grater with the steel blade. Mince the onion and mint, then add the other dressing ingredients. Pulse briefly, scraping down the sides of the bowl a couple of times. Sauté the carrots, pour on the dressing, and toss to combine.

Serves 4

38 CALORIES PER SERVING: 1 G PROTEIN, 1 G FAT, 7 G CARBOHYDRATE; 84 MG SODIUM; 0 MG CHOLESTEROL

Coleslaw with Horseradish Dressing

Forget those heavy, creamy coleslaws. This one is light and refreshing, with just enough bite to keep it interesting.

2 tablespoons	lemon juice
2 teaspoons	white vinegar
1 tablespoon	olive oil
¼ teaspoon	bottled white horseradish
¼ teaspoon	freshly ground pepper (or to taste)
½ pound	green cabbage, shredded (about 3½ cups)
1	carrot, shredded
⅓ cup	thinly sliced red onion

1. Whisk the first 5 ingredients together in a large bowl.
2. Toss in the vegetables, stir, and chill.

Serves 8

28 CALORIES PER SERVING: 1 G PROTEIN, 2 G FAT, 3 G CARBOHYDRATE; 8 MG SODIUM; 0 MG CHOLESTEROL

Horseradish

Bottled horseradish is made with oil, but the actual amount consumed is negligible since only small amounts of the horseradish itself can be eaten! You can make your own horseradish by pureeing the fresh root with a little white vinegar. For purple horseradish, include a beet, which adds color as well as sweetness and cuts back on the horseradish bite. As horseradish is exposed to air, its strength is weakened. In my family, horseradish is considered good only if it brings tears to the eyes.

Marinated Cucumber Salad

For best flavor, this salad should sit overnight before serving. It is perfect for those hot, hazy late-summer afternoons.

½ small	red onion, thinly sliced
1 tablespoon	minced fresh dill
2 tablespoons	lemon juice
½ cup	water
2 tablespoons	frozen apple juice concentrate
3	cucumbers, peeled, seeded, and sliced

1. Whisk the first 5 ingredients together in a bowl.
2. Add the cucumbers and stir until well blended.
3. Chill overnight before serving.

Serves 6

34 CALORIES PER SERVING: 1 G PROTEIN, 0 G FAT, 8 G CARBOHYDRATE;
6 MG SODIUM; 0 MG CHOLESTEROL

Cucumbers

Cucumbers are at their best when they are small, firm, and green. Large, yellowish cucumbers are usually soft-textured and have big seeds and a bitter taste. I learned this lesson after having to throw out 4 gallons of soup made from overripened cucumbers (there's no way to hide that flavor). Now I taste a little bit of each cucumber before cooking with it or adding it to a salad.

When a recipe requires seeded cucumbers, this means that the cucumber is split lengthwise and the seeds and watery membrane are scraped out with a spoon. Salads made from seeded cucumbers stay fresh longer.

Sometimes, pickling cucumbers can be found in the market. They are never waxed and don't need to be peeled or seeded. They are crunchy, full of flavor, and rarely bitter. Use them as you would the larger-sized cucumbers.

Cucumber Raita

Serve this cooling salad as an accompaniment to spicy Middle Eastern or Indian foods.

½ cup	low-fat yogurt
2 teaspoons	lemon juice
1 teaspoon	minced fresh mint
¼ teaspoon	ground cumin
1	cucumber, peeled, seeded, and diced

1. Whisk the first 4 ingredients together in a bowl.
2. Stir in the cucumber and mix well. Refrigerate about 2-3 hours, or until well chilled.

Serves 4

28 CALORIES PER SERVING: 2 G PROTEIN, 1 G FAT, 4 G CARBOHYDRATE; 21 MG SODIUM; 2 MG CHOLESTEROL

Cucumber Yogurt Salad

This is a staple at American picnics.

⅓ cup	low-fat yogurt
1 tablespoon	lemon juice
¼ teaspoon	celery seed
1 teaspoon	minced fresh dill, or ½ teaspoon dried
⅛ teaspoon	salt
⅛ teaspoon	freshly ground pepper
2	cucumbers, peeled, seeded, and thickly sliced
¼	red onion, diced (about ½ cup)

1. Whisk the first 6 ingredients together in a bowl.
2. Stir in the cucumbers and onion, and serve chilled.

Serves 5

29 CALORIES PER SERVING: 2 G PROTEIN, 0 G FAT, 5 G CARBOHYDRATE; 66 MG SODIUM; 1 MG CHOLESTEROL

Pickled Beets

For best results, make this at least a day in advance.

1 cup	apple cider vinegar
2 tablespoons	honey or malt syrup
1 cup	water
3	peppercorns
1	bay leaf
2	whole cloves
1	small onion, sliced
5 cups	beets, steamed, peeled, and sliced (about 2 bunches)

1. Bring the vinegar, sweetener, and water to a boil in a small saucepan. Add the peppercorns, bay leaf, and cloves. Simmer 10 minutes.
2. Place the sliced onion and beets in the bottom of a jar or bowl. Pour the hot liquid over the vegetables, and cover.
3. Let marinate for at least 1 day before serving.

Serves 8

42 CALORIES PER SERVING: 1 G PROTEIN, 0 G FAT, 11 G CARBOHYDRATE; 25 MG SODIUM; 0 MG CHOLESTEROL

Red and Purple Salad

Make this salad only when ripe tomatoes and fresh herbs are available. It will last several days in the refrigerator, and gets even better over time. Remove the garlic after the first day or it will overpower the rest of the flavors—and your refrigerator.

1	shallot, minced (about 1 tablespoon)
1 tablespoon	minced fresh parsley
1½ tablespoons	minced fresh basil
½	red onion, thinly sliced (about ½ cup)
1½ pounds	tomatoes, cut into wedges (4 to 6 tomatoes)
½ cup	red wine vinegar
1 tablespoon	olive oil
1 tablespoon	vegetable oil

| ¼ teaspoon | salt |
| 1 clove | garlic, peeled and crushed |

1. Toss all ingredients together.
2. Chill for at least 4 hours before serving.

Serves 8

54 CALORIES PER SERVING: 1 G PROTEIN, 4 G FAT, 6 G CARBOHYDRATE;
141 MG SODIUM; 0 MG CHOLESTEROL

Southwestern Corn Salad

I make this in the summer when I get carried away buying fresh ears
of corn at local farm stands. Since the natural sugars in fresh corn
quickly turn into starch, making the kernels tough and bland, it is best
to cook corn the day that it is brought home. Corn kernels can be
scraped off leftover ears and used for salads or put into soups or stir-
fries. In the winter, I use frozen corn.

3½ to 4 cups	corn kernels, cooked (about 4 ears)
1	bell pepper, chopped
4	scallions, sliced
4	cherry tomatoes, halved
2 teaspoons	corn oil
3 tablespoons	lime juice
3 tablespoons	minced fresh parsley or cilantro
¹⁄₁₆ to ⅛ teaspoon	cayenne pepper
⅛ teaspoon	salt

1. Toss the vegetables together in a bowl.
2. Whisk together the remaining ingredients, pour over the vegetables,
and stir until well blended.

Serves 6

113 CALORIES PER SERVING: 4 G PROTEIN, 2 G FAT, 25 G CARBOHYDRATE;
51 MG SODIUM; 0 MG CHOLESTEROL

Pommery Potato Salad

Although this recipe makes a lot and can be halved, potato salads are meant for parties and picnics. This has a shelf life of five days, so don't let the large quantity deter you.

5 cups	red bliss potatoes, cut into cubes and steamed until fork tender (about 2 pounds)
1	green bell pepper, chopped
1	red bell pepper, chopped
2 ribs	celery, chopped
6	scallions, sliced
2 tablespoons	minced fresh parsley
2 cloves	garlic
1 cup	low-fat cottage cheese
½ cup	low-fat yogurt
1 teaspoon	frozen apple juice concentrate
3 tablespoons	pommery mustard
1½ teaspoons	soy sauce
dash	paprika
dash	freshly ground pepper
½ teaspoon	celery seed
2 teaspoons	minced fresh dill, or ½ teaspoon dried

1. Allow the potatoes to cool to room temperature, and combine them with the next 5 ingredients.
2. Mince the garlic in a food processor fitted with metal blade, then add the remaining ingredients and puree until thick and smooth.
3. Pour the dressing over the vegetables, toss, and serve.

Serves 8

72 CALORIES PER SERVING: 7 G PROTEIN, 1 G FAT, 10 G CARBOHYDRATE; 291 MG SODIUM; 2 MG CHOLESTEROL

Sunburst Salad

Grain-based salads are ideal for work or travel. This one is especially filling and satisfying, with lots of fiber supplied by complex carbohydrates, fresh vegetables, and refreshing oranges.

3 cups	cooked whole grain (try wheat berries for a sweet crunch)
1	orange, cut in half crosswise, with segments removed, as you would with a grapefruit (squeeze the juice from the pulp onto the grain)
1	cucumber, peeled, seeded, and chopped
4	scallions, sliced
2 tablespoons	chopped fresh parsley
½ cup	dried fruit, soaked in hot water to soften, then sliced (try apricots and peaches)
¼ cup	toasted nuts or seeds (I prefer pepitas)
3 tablespoons	lemon juice
1 tablespoon	dijon mustard
2 tablespoons	olive oil
¼ teaspoon	ground cinnamon
1 teaspoon	chopped fresh mint, or ⅓ teaspoon dried

1. Combine the whole grain, orange, cucumber, scallions, parsley, dried fruit, and nuts.
2. Whisk together the remaining ingredients and pour over the salad. Toss to combine.
3. Allow the salad to mellow and chill for at least 1 hour before serving.

Serves 5

256 CALORIES PER SERVING: 6 G PROTEIN, 9 G FAT, 40 G CARBOHYDRATE; 45 MG SODIUM; 0 MG CHOLESTEROL

Japanese Noodle Salad

A half pound of firm tofu, cubed, can be added to this salad, which will make it a complete meal in a bowl. For those of you who can't get enough garlic and ginger, a half teaspoon of each, minced, can be added at the same time as the sesame seeds. If you like spicy foods, try a touch of Chinese hot chili paste, or sesame oil infused with hot peppers. Either udon or soba noodles can be used. Udon are mild and chewy, while soba are earthy and hearty in flavor. It's your choice.

8-ounce package	Japanese noodles
1	carrot, grated or thinly sliced
1½ cups	broccoli florets and stems (the latter peeled and sliced diagonally)
2 tablespoons	sesame oil
1 tablespoon	vegetable oil
2 tablespoons	sesame seeds
4	scallions, sliced on the diagonal
1½ tablespoons	soy sauce
1 teaspoon	lemon juice

1. Cook the noodles, then run under cool water and set aside.
2. Steam the carrot and broccoli until broccoli is bright green. Rinse the vegetables under cold running water to prevent further cooking.
3. Heat the oils in a pan until hot but not bubbling. Add the sesame seeds and stir. Remove the pan from the heat as soon as the seeds turn light brown. Stir the scallions into the hot oil; they will wilt.
4. Combine the noodles, vegetables, and scallions with oil. Add the soy sauce and lemon juice, stirring to combine.
5. Chill before serving.

Serves 6

223 CALORIES PER SERVING: 6 G PROTEIN, 9 G FAT, 30 G CARBOHYDRATE; 269 MG SODIUM; 0 MG CHOLESTEROL

Japanese Noodles

Noodle dishes are a favorite in Japan. They appear in all forms—from peasant food to elegant, gourmet dishes. Easy to prepare, filling, and gratifying, they are Japan's fast food.

The two major types of Japanese noodles are called soba and udon. Udon noodles, made from wheat flour and salt, are large and flat. Their texture, which is both chewy and soft, is like that of no other pasta.

Soba noodles are flavored; some contain spinach or tea leaves. The soba noodles available in the United States are likely to be made from buckwheat flour. When made from 100% buckwheat, they tend to have a strong, earthy flavor, and fall apart if cooked for a moment too long. Soba noodles made from a combination of wheat and buckwheat are easier to cook, have a milder though still distinctive flavor, and blend well with other ingredients.

Presto Pesto Pasta Salad

Keep pesto on hand in the refrigerator or freezer to provide the base for many soups, salads, and entrées.

1	red bell pepper, sliced julienne
1½ cups	broccoli, steamed until bright green
3 cups	cooked pasta, preferably a fat and stubby shape, like wheels or rotini
2 tablespoons	pesto (see page 117)
½ tablespoon	corn or olive oil
⅛ teaspoon	salt
¼ teaspoon	freshly ground pepper

1. Toss together the bell pepper, broccoli, and pasta.
2. Mix the pesto, oil, salt, and pepper in a small bowl. Pour over the pasta mixture and toss until evenly coated.

Serves 4

281 CALORIES PER SERVING: 10 G PROTEIN, 13 G FAT, 35 G CARBOHYDRATE; 135 MG SODIUM; 3 MG CHOLESTEROL

Toasted Quinoa Salad

The grain quinoa (pronounced keen-wa) grows in the high Andes mountains in Peru and Bolivia. Although the soil is marginal and the rainfall is sparse, the quinoa thrives.

Some have touted quinoa as the supergrain of the future, but in reality it is a food of the past. It was a staple of South Americans for centuries due to its hardy nature and nutritional content. It provides all eight essential amino acids needed by the body to build protein, in a more complete balance than most other plants. It is a good source of calcium and phosphorus. The Conquistadors knew that to conquer the Andes they had to remove quinoa from its dominance, and they did. It remained part of the peasant culture, however, and continued to be cultivated in the high reaches of the mountains. It recently has been rediscovered, and is being cultivated for a market that it has never before reached.

Quinoa grains are small and ivory-colored. When cooked, the germ layer forms a white halo around the grain. Quinoa is lighter in texture than other whole grains, which makes it similar to couscous. It adds substance without heaviness to salads and soups and has a mild but distinctive flavor, reminiscent of winter squash. If not thoroughly rinsed before cooking, it can taste soapy. Quinoa is best if dry toasted before being simmered in liquid. One of the fastest cooking grains, it is done in only 15 minutes. One cup of dry quinoa expands to almost 4 cups cooked. Although it is costly, a little goes a long way.

¾ cup	uncooked quinoa
1½ cups	water
1 cup	carrot, diced
½	red bell pepper, chopped
¼ cup	minced fresh parsley
2	scallions, sliced
½ cup	pepitas, toasted
1½ tablespoons	soy sauce
¼ cup	lemon juice
6 drops	hot pepper sauce (or to taste)
1 clove	garlic, minced

1. Rinse the quinoa. Put in a pot and dry toast until a few grains begin to pop. Add the water and bring to a boil. Cover, reduce heat, and simmer for 15 minutes, or until the quinoa has absorbed all the liquid. Remove from heat and let stand for 10 minutes. Fluff with a fork.

2. Mix the carrot, bell pepper, parsley, scallions, and pepitas in a large bowl. When quinoa has cooled add it to the bowl and combine.
3. Whisk together the soy sauce, lemon juice, hot sauce, and garlic. Pour over other ingredients and toss to mix.

Serves 5

140 CALORIES PER SERVING: 5 G PROTEIN, 3 G FAT, 25 G CARBOHYDRATE; 317 MG SODIUM; 0 MG CHOLESTEROL

Bulgur Wheat Salad

This is an ideal solution to the recurring problem of what to take to the office for lunch—although you might want to reduce the garlic . . . .

2 cups	boiling water
1 cup	uncooked bulgur wheat
⅓ cup	lemon juice
½ to 1 teaspoon	soy sauce (or to taste)
dash	cayenne pepper
2 cloves	garlic, minced
1	tomato, diced
1 cup	minced scallions
3 tablespoons	minced fresh parsley
2 tablespoons	minced fresh mint leaves, or 2 teaspoons dried
2 tablespoons	olive oil
	romaine lettuce leaves (optional)

1. Pour the water over the bulgur wheat and let rest for 30–45 minutes. (Bulgur wheat varies in coarseness. The larger the grain, the longer it needs to soak; some needs only 10 minutes in lukewarm water.)
2. Combine the rest of the ingredients, then mix with the softened bulgur and serve on a bed of lettuce, if desired.

Serves 4

246 CALORIES PER SERVING: 5 G PROTEIN, 8 G FAT, 42 G CARBOHYDRATE; 52 MG SODIUM; 0 MG CHOLESTEROL

Wheat Berry and Barley Salad

Wheat berries are sweet and crunchy, while barley is soft and chewy, and together they make a perfect combination. A light dressing keeps this salad from being too heavy.

½ cup	uncooked wheat berries
½ cup	uncooked barley
3 cups	cold water
3	scallions, sliced
½	green bell pepper, chopped
1	carrot, chopped or grated
6	radishes, sliced
¼ cup	chopped fresh parsley
3 tablespoons	olive oil
2 tablespoons	red wine vinegar
2 tablespoons	lemon juice
1 teaspoon	fresh dill weed or ¼ teaspoon dried
⅛ teaspoon	freshly ground pepper
6 drops	hot pepper sauce
½ to 1 teaspoon	soy sauce (or to taste)

1. Simmer the wheat berries and barley together, covered, in a pot with the water for about 1 hour, until all of the water is absorbed and the grains are tender.
2. Cool the grains, then add the next 5 ingredients, stirring to blend.
3. Whisk together the remaining ingredients, pour over the salad, mix well, and serve.

Serves 5

185 CALORIES PER SERVING: 3 G PROTEIN, 9 G FAT, 25 G CARBOHYDRATE; 44 MG SODIUM; 0 MG CHOLESTEROL

Red Lentil Salad

Most bean recipes are time-consuming to make. This one is not; the red lentils cook in less than 5 minutes. Serve it as a cool summer salad, or as a hearty lunch in the fall.

1 cup	red lentils (use the larger size)
3 cups	cold water
2 tablespoons	olive oil
4 teaspoons	red wine vinegar
1 tablespoon	balsamic vinegar
¼ teaspoon	salt (or to taste)
⅛ teaspoon	freshly ground pepper
8 drops	hot pepper sauce
3	scallions, sliced
1	medium cucumber, peeled, seeded, and chopped, or 2 pickling cucumbers

1. Rinse the lentils and check for stones. Bring the water to a boil and add the lentils.
2. Reduce the heat and simmer for about 4 minutes. If allowed to cook too long, they will turn to mush; too little time and they will be hard. Keep an eye on the pot. A foam will rise to the surface of the water, but ignore it.
3. As soon as the lentils soften, pour them into a mesh strainer (a colander's holes are too big) and rinse very gently with cold water until cool. This keeps them from becoming a sticky mass.
4. Combine the remaining ingredients, toss with the lentils, and serve.

Serves 6

156 CALORIES PER SERVING: 9 G PROTEIN, 5 G FAT, 20 G CARBOHYDRATE;
93 MG SODIUM; 0 MG CHOLESTEROL

All-Season Black Bean Salad

You can find the ingredients for this salad year-round. The ingredient list is long, but the preparation is simple.

3 cups	cooked black beans
1	red bell pepper, chopped
½	green bell pepper, chopped
¼	red onion, chopped
2	scallions, sliced (use as much of the green tops as are crisp)
1 rib	celery, finely chopped
1	orange
1½ tablespoons	lemon juice
1 teaspoon	olive oil
1½ tablespoons	orange juice
¼ teaspoon	hot pepper sauce
¼ teaspoon	salt
½ teaspoon	ground cumin
¼ teaspoon	ground coriander

1. In a large bowl, combine the first 6 ingredients, tossing well.
2. Cut the orange in half and scoop out the segments, as you would with a grapefruit. Add the segments to the bean mixture and squeeze the juice from the orange into the bowl. Take care not to drop in any seeds.
3. Whisk together (or shake in a glass jar) the remaining ingredients, pour over the salad, and toss to coat.

Serves 6

144 CALORIES PER SERVING: 8 G PROTEIN, 1 G FAT, 26 G CARBOHYDRATE; 96 MG SODIUM; 0 MG CHOLESTEROL

Many Bean Salad

Beans of any type and any combination will work here, but because beans have different cooking times, cook them separately.

1 cup	cooked pinto beans
1 cup	cooked chick-peas
1 cup	cooked white beans
1 to 2 cups	sliced fresh green beans, steamed

½ cup	thinly sliced red onion
2	scallions, sliced
2 tablespoons	minced fresh parsley
1 small clove	garlic, minced
¼ cup	red wine vinegar
2 tablespoons	olive oil
1 to 2 teaspoons	frozen apple juice concentrate
¼ teaspoon	freshly ground pepper
½ teaspoon	salt

good!

1. In a large bowl, combine pinto beans, chick-peas, white beans, green beans, onion, scallions, and parsley.
2. In a separate bowl, whisk together the remaining ingredients, pour over beans, and toss to coat.

Serves 6

173 CALORIES PER SERVING: 9 G PROTEIN, 5 G FAT, 25 G CARBOHYDRATE; 182 MG SODIUM; 0 MG CHOLESTEROL

Blissful Tuna Salad

Make up a batch on Sunday night, then use as a brown bag lunch for the work week.

6½-ounce can	tuna, packed in water
⅔ pound	red bliss potatoes, cut into ½ inch cubes, then steamed until tender
½ pound	green beans, trimmed, cut in half, and steamed until bright green and still crisp
½ cup	thinly sliced red onion
2 tablespoons	minced fresh parsley
1	tomato, cut into 8 wedges, each wedge halved
½ cup	vinaigrette of your choice

1. Drain the tuna, and toss all the ingredients together in a bowl.
2. Chill several hours to allow the potatoes to absorb the flavors.

Serves 6

152 CALORIES PER SERVING: 11 G PROTEIN, 5 G FAT, 17 G CARBOHYDRATE; 206 MG SODIUM; 16 MG CHOLESTEROL

Ocean and Grape Salad

This is an appetizing, cool salad for a sultry summer day.

1 pound	poached white-fleshed fish, such as pollock, scrod, catfish (see page 94 for poaching fish)
¾ cup	low-fat cottage cheese
¼ cup	low-fat yogurt
2 teaspoons	sherry
1½ cups	halved seedless grapes
1 tablespoon	minced fresh dill
⅛ teaspoon	freshly ground pepper
⅛ teaspoon	salt
	fresh lemon juice
	lemon wedges

1. Break the fish into bite-sized flakes.
2. Puree the cottage cheese, yogurt, and sherry to the consistency of mayonnaise. (This is best done in a food processor fitted with metal blade.)
3. Stir together the grapes, cottage cheese mixture, dill, and seasonings. Add the fish.
4. Serve on a bed of leafy lettuce, squeeze lemon juice over each portion, and garnish with lemon wedges. (The fresh lemon is a necessity for the flavoring of this—it is not just a garnish!)

Serves 4

238 CALORIES PER SERVING: 33 G PROTEIN, 3 G FAT, 13 G CARBOHYDRATE; 364 MG SODIUM; 84 MG CHOLESTEROL

Chicken and Artichoke Heart Salad

Every take-out food counter, whether it be a supermarket deli or a fancy gourmet shop, has a best-selling chicken salad. If I had a deli, this would be my signature chicken salad. (Pasta can be used instead of brown rice, if desired.)

½ pound	skinless, boneless chicken breast, poached and cubed
8-ounce can	artichoke hearts, packed in water (6 artichokes)

½	red bell pepper, cut julienne
1 rib	celery, cut on the diagonal
¼ cup	thinly sliced red onion
1 cup	cooked long-grain brown rice
1 tablespoon	dried tarragon
½ cup	Red Wine Vinaigrette (see page 30)

1. Gently stir the chicken, vegetables, rice, and tarragon together.
2. Pour on the dressing and toss to coat.
3. Refrigerate several hours to allow the flavors to meld.

Serves 6

147 CALORIES PER SERVING: 12 G PROTEIN, 6 G FAT, 12 G CARBOHYDRATE;
151 MG SODIUM; 27 MG CHOLESTEROL

How to Poach Chicken

Leftover, dried, or overcooked chicken can ruin even the best-dressed salad, so I make sure to used freshly poached chicken. Although both poaching and boiling rely on moist heat, they are not interchangeable techniques. Boiled food is immersed in highly agitated liquid. Poached food is partially submerged in liquid that is gently simmering, with only little bubbles rising to the surface. Poaching, obviously, is a gentler form of cooking.

When water is the cooking medium it imparts no flavor; when the liquid is stock or wine, or when there are herbs and spices in the pot, subtle seasonings are imparted to the food. Poaching simmers food just to the point of doneness. For chicken, that means that the texture is firm, not rubbery or tough.

To poach chicken breasts, use a pot or pan with a close-fitting lid. The heavier the pot, the better, because thick-bottomed pots retain heat and cook foods evenly. Bring the liquid to a simmer, then place the chicken in it. Cover the pan and simmer for 7 minutes. Turn the meat over, and simmer for 10 minutes longer. If there is a lot of chicken in the pot, or if the chicken has bones, cook it for another 10 minutes, then turn off the heat and let the chicken rest in the hot liquid for 20 minutes. The end product will be plump, moist pieces of chicken that are thoroughly cooked and perfect for chicken salads.

Curried Chicken Salad

Since no curry powder is alike, you might want to add only half the amount called for, then taste to decide how much more to mix in. This salad will remain fresh for up to four days in the refrigerator. With time, it will become a darker yellow and liquid may separate from the dressing. This can be stirred back in.

1¼ pounds	skinless, boneless chicken breast, poached (about 4 cups, cubed)
1	green bell pepper, chopped
½ cup	diced celery
⅔ cup	thinly sliced red onion
½ cup	raisins
2	apples
2	teaspoons lemon juice
1 cup	low-fat cottage cheese
¾ cup	low-fat yogurt
½ teaspoon	turmeric
1 to 2 tablespoons	curry powder
⅛ teaspoon	cayenne pepper (or to taste)
1 teaspoon	frozen apple juice concentrate

1. Toss the cubed chicken with the bell pepper, celery, onion, and raisins.
2. Cut the apples into cored wedges, and then halve. Toss with the lemon juice to prevent browning. Add the apples to the chicken.
3. In a food processor fitted with metal blade, puree the remaining ingredients until the dressing is smooth and thick.
4. Pour the dressing over the salad and toss to coat.

Serves 8

209 CALORIES PER SERVING: 27 G PROTEIN, 3 G FAT, 17 G CARBOHYDRATE; 193 MG SODIUM; 63 MG CHOLESTEROL

Curry Powder

In general, spices come from seeds, and herbs from the leafy parts of plants. Although curry powder is often considered a spice, it is made from more than one plant and contains both herbs and spices—as few as five, or as many as fifteen, ranging from mouth-burning hot to mildly sweet. There are numerous curry powders on the market, each one different from the next; consequently, you might dislike one, but love another.

Commercial curry powders are convenient, but rarely as good as those made at home. Making your own blend is time-consuming, however, and it can be hard to find the whole spices. One way to compromise is to start with a good-quality commercial brand as a base, then add a couple of other spices as you cook. In this way you create a unique flavor designed for each recipe. Some of the herbs and spices that complement commercial curry powders are cinnamon, cardamom, cumin, coriander, cayenne, turmeric, oregano, chili powder, garlic, ginger, and mustard seed. Balance the sweeter ones (such as cinnamon and cardamom) with the hotter ones (such as chili powder and cayenne).

Almost all curries include turmeric, a mild, slightly bitter spice that turns foods yellow, and thus is called "poor man's saffron." Caution is needed when cooking with turmeric, because as the food becomes hotter on the stove, the yellow becomes brighter, often giving an unnaturally colorful effect. Be conservative with the other seasonings as well until you become familiar with them.

Indonesian Rice Salad

This can stand on its own without the chicken or tofu—just reduce the amount of dressing or add more vegetables, such as snow peas.

½ pound	skinless, boneless chicken breast or tofu
1 recipe	Indonesian Sauce (see page 84)
½ cup	bean sprouts
1 cup	cooked brown rice
2	scallions, sliced
½	red bell pepper, chopped
½ cup	peas
8-ounce can	unsweetened pineapple chunks, drained
½ cup	sliced water chestnuts (or jicama—a vegetable that tastes like fresh chestnuts—peeled, sliced, and cut into bite-sized pieces)
2 tablespoons	orange juice
½ teaspoon	soy sauce

1. Cut the chicken or tofu into cubes. Reserve 2 tablespoons of the Indonesian sauce, and marinate the chicken for at least 1 hour; the tofu overnight. If using tofu, place it (after marinating) on a baking sheet lined with parchment paper and bake in a 425 degree F oven for 15 minutes. Shake the pan several times during cooking to loosen the cubes. Turn the cubes over and bake another 15 minutes, or until crispy. If using chicken, bake in a similar fashion, but at 350 degrees F for about 20 minutes.
2. Combine the bean sprouts, rice, scallions, bell pepper, peas, pineapple, and water chestnuts. When the tofu or chicken cools, add that as well.
3. Whisk together the reserved 2 tablespoons Indonesian Sauce, the orange juice, and soy sauce. Pour over the salad and stir gently to mix well.

Serves 4

260 CALORIES PER SERVING: 11 G PROTEIN, 7 G FAT, 42 G CARBOHYDRATE; 291 MG SODIUM; 0 MG CHOLESTEROL

Spanish Rice Salad

This zesty salad has about 3 ounces of meat per serving. Vegetarians can make it with tofu or tempeh.

1 cup	long-grain brown rice
¾ cup	tomato juice
1½ cups	water
¼ cup	red wine vinegar
¼ cup	olive oil
¼ teaspoon	hot pepper sauce (or to taste)
1 teaspoon	dried thyme
¼ teaspoon	paprika
¼ teaspoon	garlic powder (or 1 small clove, minced)
¼ teaspoon	salt
1	green bell pepper, chopped
1	red bell pepper, chopped
¼	red onion, thinly sliced
2	tomatoes, chopped
¼ cup	minced fresh parsley
1 pound	skinless, boneless chicken breast, poached and cut into bite-sized chunks

1. Cook the rice, covered, in ½ cup of the tomato juice and the water for 40–45 minutes. It will be sticky, but more flavorful than rice cooked in water only. When done, cool the rice to room temperature.
2. Whisk together the vinegar, oil, remaining tomato juice, hot sauce, thyme, paprika, garlic, and salt.
3. Combine the rice, bell peppers, onion, tomatoes, parsley, and chicken. Pour the dressing over all, toss to coat, and serve immediately or chill.

Serves 6

346 CALORIES PER SERVING: 27 G PROTEIN, 13 G FAT, 31 G CARBOHYDRATE; 261 MG SODIUM; 64 MG CHOLESTEROL

SOUPS

Making soup is a creative process. If you've always wanted to cut loose in the kitchen, this is the dish to start with. First of all, many soups can be served either hot or cold, such as my Gingery Almond Carrot Soup, for example. Try it both ways, and with or without yogurt. Each time you make Melon-Berry Swirl, try a different berry. Use No-Bones Chicken Soup as a springboard to homemade vegetable soups, filling it with mushrooms one time, and sweet potatoes and rutabagas another. Puree it. Leave it chunky. Add chopped celery leaves. It's hard to overcook soup, and hard to season it incorrectly. If a flavor gets too strong for your liking, just add more of the base until the soup tastes right. And if you end up making more than expected, freeze half in serving-sized portions. Homemade soup is a wonderful dinner to come home to—and a welcoming spur-of-the-moment dish for unexpected company.

Garlic and Dill Tomato Soup

A quick, easy, and tasty soup that fits the bill any time of the year. Serve hot or chilled and top with low-fat yogurt and sliced scallions or sprigs of fresh dill weed.

1½ cups	minced onion (1 Spanish onion)
3 large	cloves garlic, minced
2 tablespoons	vegetable oil
6 cups	canned tomatoes, coarsely chopped
2 cups	liquid from the canned tomatoes, or tomato juice if necessary
1 tablespoon	frozen apple juice concentrate
dash	freshly ground pepper
1 tablespoon	fresh dill weed, or 1 teaspoon dried

1. Sauté the onion and garlic in the oil until the onion becomes translucent and slightly brown at the edges. Do this over a low heat so the garlic doesn't burn.
2. Combine with remaining ingredients in a soup pot and simmer 30 minutes. Serve hot or chill.

Serves 8

89 CALORIES PER SERVING: 3 G PROTEIN, 4 G FAT, 13 G CARBOHYDRATE; 514 MG SODIUM; 0 MG CHOLESTEROL

Gazpacho

I used to make this soup when I was a chef at a Harvard Square cafe. I had customers who would order two bowls at a time, which I considered the ultimate compliment. If you're in a rush, or really dislike cutting and chopping, all of the ingredients can be pureed. The resulting soup will be good, but if the directions below are followed, it will be even better. The texture will be crunchy and smooth, the colors will be beautiful, and the flavors perfectly harmonized.

1 quart	tomato juice
1	lemon, juiced
2	limes, juiced
2 tablespoons	red wine vinegar
1 teaspoon	frozen apple juice concentrate
14-ounce can	whole tomatoes (or 3 very ripe, flavorful fresh tomatoes)
2 to 3	fresh tomatoes
½	red onion, minced
1	green bell pepper, minced
1	cucumber, peeled, seeded, and minced
1	cucumber, peeled and seeded
1 clove	garlic, minced
1 tablespoon	dried basil
2 teaspoons	dried tarragon
⅓ cup	minced fresh parsley
2 tablespoons	minced fresh chives
½ teaspoon	paprika
6 drops	hot pepper sauce
2 teaspoons	soy sauce

1. In a large bowl, combine the tomato juice, lemon and lime juices, vinegar, and apple juice concentrate.
2. Pour the juice from the canned tomatoes into the bowl, straining and discarding any seeds. Remove seeds from the canned tomatoes by holding them under gently running water and rinsing out the seeds. Add the tomatoes to the bowl, breaking them apart with your hands. (Canned tomatoes are so soft that they don't need chopping.)
3. Seed, then mince the fresh tomatoes. Add to the bowl, along with the onion, bell pepper, and minced cucumber.
4. Puree the second cucumber with the garlic, and add to the soup. This contributes body.

5. Stir in the remaining ingredients, chill overnight, then season to taste.

Serves 10

51 CALORIES PER SERVING: 2 G PROTEIN, 0 G FAT, 12 G CARBOHYDRATE; 430 MG SODIUM; 0 MG CHOLESTEROL

Cucumber Yogurt Soup

This chilled soup makes a nice addition to a summer buffet or a Sunday brunch.

1 clove	garlic
3	cucumbers, peeled, seeded, and cut into large chunks
¼ cup	water
1	cucumber, peeled, seeded, and minced
3 cups	low-fat yogurt (2 pounds)
1½ tablespoons	minced fresh dill
1½ teaspoons	minced fresh mint
⅛ teaspoon	salt
⅛ teaspoon	freshly ground pepper
3	scallions, minced, or 2 tablespoons minced fresh chives scallions, fresh mint, chives, or dill as garnish

1. Mince the garlic in a blender or food processor fitted with metal blade. Drop in the 3 cucumbers, pour in the water, and puree.
2. Whisk together the pureed ingredients, the minced cucumber, yogurt, herbs, seasonings, and scallions.
3. Serve cold, with sliced scallions, mint, chives, or dill as a garnish.

Serves 6

100 CALORIES PER SERVING: 7 G PROTEIN, 2 G FAT, 14 G CARBOHYDRATE; 133 MG SODIUM; 7 MG CHOLESTEROL

Melon-Berry Swirl

This dramatic and extravagant looking soup takes only minutes to prepare.

2 pounds	melon meat, preferably yellow or green in color, such as canary or honeydew (a 4-pound melon yields about 3 pounds usable fruit)
1 teaspoon	frozen apple juice concentrate
¼ teaspoon	ground cinnamon
⅛ teaspoon	ground cloves
2 teaspoons	lemon juice
3 tablespoons	minced fresh mint
2 cups	berries (raspberries, strawberries, blueberries)
2 teaspoons	lemon juice
⅓ cup	low-fat yogurt
	fresh mint leaves for garnish

1. Puree the first 6 ingredients, then chill.
2. Puree the berries, lemon juice, and yogurt, and chill also.
3. Just prior to serving, pour the melon mixture into soup bowls, filling them no more than ⅔ of the way.
4. Pour the berry puree into the center of the soup bowls.
5. Create a swirling pattern by mixing the two purees using one circular motion with a spoon. Garnish with fresh mint leaves.

Serves 6

84 CALORIES PER SERVING: 2 G PROTEIN, 1 G FAT, 20 G CARBOHYDRATE;
24 MG SODIUM; 1 MG CHOLESTEROL

Gingery Almond Carrot Soup

Fresh ginger always perks me up, and it adds just the right touch to this colorful, invigorating soup.

1½ pounds	carrots, peeled and shredded
1 cup	white wine
3 cups	water
1 tablespoon	lemon juice
½ small	yellow onion, chopped
1 clove	garlic, minced
1 teaspoon	peeled and grated fresh ginger
2 tablespoons	almonds or almond pieces
	oil to coat bottom of sauté pan
¼ teaspoon	curry powder
1½ teaspoons	salt
¼ teaspoon	freshly ground pepper
	sliced, toasted almonds for garnish

1. Simmer the carrots, wine, water, and lemon juice until the carrots are tender, about 15 minutes.
2. Meanwhile, sauté the onion, garlic, ginger, and almonds in the oil until the onion softens and the garlic turns golden. Take care not to scorch. Stir in the spices.
3. Add the sautéed mixture to the carrots and puree until smooth.
4. Serve hot or chilled. Garnish with sliced, toasted almonds.

Serves 8

75 CALORIES PER SERVING: 1 G PROTEIN, 2 G FAT, 10 G CARBOHYDRATE; 448 MG SODIUM; 0 MG CHOLESTEROL

Borscht

Nothing compares to the sweet-and-sour taste of borscht. It is cool and refreshing in the summer, warming and satisfying in the winter. If fresh beets are unavailable, substitute canned, shoestring unsweetened beets.

1	all-purpose potato, peeled and cubed
1½ pounds	beets, peeled and grated (use a food processor fitted with metal blade for this task and wear rubber gloves to keep your hands from getting stained)
1	yellow onion, chopped
6	cups water
2	bay leaves
4	peppercorns
2	tomatoes, peeled, seeded, and chopped (see page 63)
1 tablespoon	tomato paste
2 tablespoons	lemon juice
1 teaspoon	vinegar (white or cider)
2 tablespoons	honey
2 teaspoons	salt
	low-fat yogurt as garnish

1. Bring the potato, beets, onion, and water to a boil. Add the bay leaves and peppercorns, and simmer, covered, for 45 minutes.
2. Add the remaining ingredients, except yogurt, and simmer for 30 minutes longer. Serve with a dollop of yogurt.

Serves 8

72 CALORIES PER SERVING: 2 G PROTEIN, 0 G FAT, 17 G CARBOHYDRATE; 580 MG SODIUM; 0 MG CHOLESTEROL

Peeling and Seeding Tomatoes

The skin and seeds are the least appealing parts of a tomato. Although removing them is a hassle, the difference in appearance, texture, and flavor in a recipe makes the effort worthwhile.

Raw tomatoes are difficult and time-consuming to peel with a paring knife, but a brief dunk into boiling water makes their skins slip right off. Bring a pot of water to a boil—large enough so that the tomatoes won't be crowded. Cut out the cores and slash an X (not too deep) in the opposite end. Drop the tomatoes into the pot and immerse only until the skin starts to peel away at the slash. Remove quickly and drop them into a bowl of cold water. (A wire mesh basket simplifies this task for the tomatoes can be immersed and then removed all at once. If you don't have a wire basket, use a slotted spoon.) Once the tomatoes are cool enough to handle, grasp the peel and pull it off. Then cut the tomatoes in half across their equators, which exposes all of the pockets with their seeds. Gently squeeze the tomato and use your fingers to remove the seeds.

Stock

When a cooking liquid needs more than just plain water, this is the time for stocks. Stocks, or broths, are easy to make. Just as tea bags are used to infuse flavor into water, so are vegetables, herbs, spices, and sometimes meats used to impart flavor to cooking liquids. And as with tea bags, these stock ingredients are tossed out before the stock is used or stored.

In a low-fat kitchen, stocks are an especially important item in the pantry. Stock will not make a recipe taste as if it has butter or cream in it, but those ingredients will not be missed if a flavorful stock is used. (Some soups taste fine without stocks, and there are several such recipes in this book.)

Stocks are not just for soup making. They can be used for cooking grains, for sautéing vegetables, and for simmering beans.

Whenever plain water is called for, stock often can be substituted, and the result is usually a richer, fuller flavor.

Fresh vegetable stock can be kept in the refrigerator for 5 days. Chicken stock, however, goes bad quickly. If it has been refrigerated for more than a day, bring it to a rolling boil for 5 minutes before using it.

Luckily, stock freezes well. If you make up a couple of big batches of stock and freeze it, you will have a supply all year. Store stocks in containers of different sizes. Keep some in 2-cup containers for cooking grains, and store larger amounts for soups. You can also pour some into an ice cube tray. Once frozen, store the cubes in freezer bags, then pull out 1 or 2 for sautés or whenever you need small amounts.

Canned stocks are convenient but inferior to homemade. They often are overly salty or sweet, or contain MSG, unnatural flavors, or preservatives. There are a few exceptions, my favorite being Hain's No-Salt Added Chicken Broth, which is sold through natural food stores. All canned stocks have a layer of fat on the surface. Remove it with a spoon before using. Because canned stocks are strong, they can be diluted with water.

Making Stocks

A vegetable stock is a slightly sweet, mild-tasting liquid, with no overpowering flavors. Chicken stock is similar, but richer. The recipes in this book yield consistent products, but you can also create your own versions. As long as the end result is a pleasant tasting liquid for cooking, the exact formulation is not important. There are, however, some rules of thumb to follow.

Vegetables must be fresh and clean. If they are not fit to eat, they are not fit for the stock pot. Stock is not a way to get rid of old, bruised, or rotten food.

Most stocks should have a base of onions, celery, and carrots. I like a moderate amount of garlic, too. Parsley, peppercorns, and herbs can also be used. The depth and intensity of the stock depend on what is put in. It can be as simple or complex as you like.

Vegetables can be left whole, but will yield more flavor if cut into pieces. If vegetable skins are bitter, they should be peeled and discarded. Onion skins can be left on to contribute a golden color to the stock.

Tomatoes are too acidic for stock, and members of the cabbage family, including cauliflower and broccoli, make stock useful only for cabbage soup. Mushroom stems, scallions, turnips, and parsnips are all welcome additions, as are yams, if a sweet stock is desired.

Stocks become more complex when herbs, fresh or dried, are simmered along with the vegetables. Almost any combination can be used, but take care not to overdo. To keep dry herbs from floating on the surface, tie them into a small cheesecloth sack called a bouquet garni. Fresh herbs can be cooked loose in the pot.

Vegetable Stock

This recipe makes a light broth that is excellent for cooking rice and other grains. No analysis has been included, for the amount of calories, protein, fat, carbohydrates, sodium, and cholesterol are all minimal.

2	carrots, peeled
1 small	onion, outside skin removed
1	leek, washed well (use everything but the topmost leaves)
3	celery stalks
1 large handful	fresh parsley
1 clove	garlic
¼ teaspoon	dried thyme
¼ teaspoon	dried rosemary
½ teaspoon	dried winter savory, or sage
2	peppercorns
4 quarts	cold water

1. Wash the vegetables well, and cut into large chunks.
2. Put the herbs and peppercorns into a bouquet garni bag, or tie up in a piece of cheesecloth. (This keeps them from floating on the surface, and also makes them easier to remove later.)
3. Put all of the ingredients into a large pot and bring to a boil. Reduce the heat and simmer, uncovered, for 45 minutes.
4. Discard the vegetables. Strain the broth through cheesecloth to remove sediment, and store in the refrigerator or freezer.

Yields 10 cups

Chicken Stock

An analysis is not included since the kind and quantity of ingredients may vary. Take care to skim off the fat that rises to the top and you will eliminate the majority of fat from the recipe.

4-pound	chicken, giblets removed, or an equivalent amount of chicken bones from a carcass (I save and freeze chicken backs from quartered birds, and breast bones that I have removed)
5 quarts	cold water
½ large	onion, cut into quarters
1	leek, sliced in half and washed thoroughly
2 ribs	celery
1	carrot
½ cup	cold water
4 cloves	garlic, skins intact
1 bunch	fresh parsley
2	bay leaves
3	peppercorns
1 teaspoon	dried thyme
½ teaspoon	dried rosemary

1. Place the chicken and 5 quarts cold water in a nonreactive pot. Bring to a rolling boil and cook at a fast bubble for 20 minutes, skimming the foam off the top.
2. Add the remaining ingredients to the pot and simmer for 1 hour, uncovered.
3. Remove the chicken from the pot, pull meat off the bones, and reserve the meat for other purposes, such as chicken noodle soup.
4. Return the bones to the pot and simmer, uncovered, 2 more hours.
5. Strain the stock through cheesecloth or a sieve. Discard the vegetables and bones.
6. Store the stock overnight in the refrigerator. Fat will rise to the surface and solidify. Skim this off and throw out. Strain the stock again to insure that all the fat and sediments have been removed.

Yields 12 cups

No-Bones Chicken Soup

This is faster to prepare than the soup your grandmother used to make, but it's still nourishing and reassuring. I try to keep serving-sized portions on hand in the freezer.

1 clove	garlic, minced
2 ribs	celery, chopped (include the leaves, if possible)
1	yellow onion, chopped
1	large carrot, chopped
½ tablespoon	olive oil
½ pound	skinless, boneless chicken breast, cubed
1 tablespoon	minced fresh parsley
2 teaspoons	minced fresh dill, or 1 teaspoon dried
4 cups	chicken stock
½ teaspoon	salt
½ teaspoon	freshly ground pepper
1 cup	cooked brown rice (for a fancy soup try wild rice), or other cooked grain or pasta
½ cup	peas

1. Sauté the garlic, celery, onion, and carrot in the oil in a soup pot. Cook over low heat for about 10 minutes until the onion becomes soft and clear in color. Between stirrings, keep the lid on the pot. Add a touch of chicken stock if there's not enough oil to keep the vegetables from sticking.
2. Make sure that the chicken is trimmed of all fat, otherwise the soup will foam and need to be skimmed. Put the chicken into the pot and cook for 1 to 2 minutes until the outside of the chicken begins to turn white.
3. Add the herbs, stock, salt, pepper, and rice or other grain. Simmer for 30 minutes, or longer if possible. If using pasta, add it 10 minutes before serving or it will get mushy; add the peas during the last 5 minutes of cooking so they remain bright green.

Serves 6

110 CALORIES PER SERVING: 11 G PROTEIN, 2 G FAT, 11 G CARBOHYDRATE; 227 MG SODIUM; 24 MG CHOLESTEROL

Potato-Leek Soup

Peasant-style leek and potato soup and the aristocratic chilled vichyssoise are one and the same. Served hot or cold, this is a simple, smooth, satisfying soup. Instead of high-fat cream, stir in fromage blanc—a no-fat, no-salt fresh cheese similar in consistency to sour cream. Its thick texture makes it a better choice than low-fat milk for the health-conscious cook. Packaged in a plastic cup that looks like a sour cream container, it can be found in some supermarkets and natural food stores. If it is unavailable, try low-fat evaporated milk or low-fat yogurt. Or leave out the dairy entirely. I like it that way. This soup is especially easy to make. Instead of cubing the potatoes, shred them in a food processor, then simmer everything together. Sautéing is not necessary.

3 cups	minced leeks, white and light green parts
4 cups	peeled, shredded all-purpose potatoes
6 cups	stock (vegetable or chicken)
½ to 1 teaspoon	salt
1 tablespoon	chopped fresh chives
1 tablespoon	chopped fresh parsley
	freshly ground pepper to taste
½ cup	fromage blanc or low-fat yogurt (optional)

1. Make sure that the leeks are washed well before mincing them. Simmer the leeks, potatoes, stock, and salt in a pot for 30 minutes. Add the chives and parsley. Cook for 10 minutes longer.
2. Stir in the pepper and dairy, if you like. Season to taste. Serve immediately or chill.

Serves 10

70 CALORIES PER SERVING: 2 G PROTEIN, 0 G FAT, 15 G CARBOHYDRATE; 124 MG SODIUM; 1 MG CHOLESTEROL

Black Bean Soup

A classic favorite, this soup is tart, spicy, and chunky. Serve with a green salad for a hearty lunch or dinner.

3 cups	dried black beans (about 1 pound), soaked overnight in water to cover
8 cups	water or stock
2	bay leaves
2	carrots, chopped
2 ribs	celery, chopped
1	medium Spanish onion, chopped
6 cloves	garlic, minced
2	limes, juiced
1 tablespoon	ground coriander
1½ teaspoons	salt
1 tablespoon	dried oregano
½ to 1 teaspoon	hot pepper sauce
¼ teaspoon	cayenne pepper
2 teaspoons	ground cumin
2 tablespoons	minced fresh parsley
¼ cup	sherry
	low-fat yogurt and scallions for garnish

1. Drain the beans from the soaking liquid, and put them into a large, heavy pot. Add the water, bay leaves, carrots, celery, and onion.
2. Bring to a boil, reduce to a simmer, cover, and cook for 1 hour.
3. Add the next 9 ingredients and simmer for 45 minutes longer, or until the beans are soft. (At this stage, half of the soup can be pureed if desired.)
4. Fifteen minutes before serving, add the sherry.
5. Garnish with a spoonful of low-fat yogurt and sliced green scallions. Serve chilled in the summer, and piping hot in the winter.

Serves 10

231 CALORIES PER SERVING: 14 G PROTEIN, 1 G FAT, 42 G CARBOHYDRATE; 336 MG SODIUM; 0 MG CHOLESTEROL

Split Pea Soup

Split pea soup is a trustworthy friend in the winter. It is easy to make (these dried beans don't need soaking) and freezes well. Buy split peas that look fresh. They should be bright green and free from dust. Good quality peas are the secret of this soup.

8 cups	water or stock
2 cups	split peas, rinsed
2	bay leaves
2 cloves	garlic, minced
1 rib	celery, chopped
2	carrots, peeled and chopped
1	leek, thoroughly washed and minced
1 tablespoon	corn oil
1 medium	all-purpose potato, peeled and cubed
2 tablespoons	minced fresh parsley
¼ teaspoon	dried thyme
½ teaspoon	dried marjoram
1 to 1½ tablespoons	soy sauce, or to taste
	freshly ground pepper to taste

1. Bring the water to a boil in a pot. Add the split peas and bay leaves. Cover and simmer for 30 minutes, stirring occasionally.
2. Meanwhile, sauté the garlic, celery, carrots, and leek in the corn oil over low heat until they soften. Add the sautéed vegetables, potato, herbs, soy sauce, and pepper to the pot, and simmer, uncovered, for another 20 minutes, stirring occasionally.

Serves 10

172 CALORIES PER SERVING: 10 G PROTEIN, 2 G FAT, 30 G CARBOHYDRATE; 120 MG SODIUM; 0 MG CHOLESTEROL

Mushroom Barley Soup

A hearty soup with robust flavor and aroma. Barley absorbs liquid and will continue to expand like a sponge for hours after the soup is cooked. By the second day you might have to thin this with stock if you want soup and not stew.

3 large cloves	garlic, minced
1 medium	onion, chopped (about ⅔ cup)
1½ cups	sherry
1 pound	mushrooms, sliced (about 5 cups)
8 cups	stock
⅔ cup	barley
2 tablespoons	soy sauce
¼ cup	minced fresh parsley
	freshly ground pepper to taste
2 tablespoons	miso (if unavailable, use 1 more tablespoon soy sauce)

1. Over low heat, sauté the garlic and onion in some sherry until the onion softens. This can be done in a thick-bottomed soup pot. Continue to add sherry as needed until the onion becomes soft and translucent. Cover the pan between stirrings.
2. Add the mushrooms and remaining sherry, cover, and cook until the mushrooms are wilted and soft. Stir once or twice.
3. Pour in the stock and add remaining ingredients, except the miso. Simmer, covered, for 1½ hours.
4. Mix the miso with ½ cup of the hot broth and stir until smooth. Pour into soup and cook for 15 more minutes.

Time saver: This is a long-cooking soup, but there is a short-cut. Use precooked barley or other precooked grain (I try to keep some on hand in my freezer). Follow steps 1 and 2, then add 2 cups cooked grain and only 5 cups stock. Simmer with the remaining ingredients. It will be ready in 15 minutes, but like many hearty soups, it benefits from a longer cooking time.

Serves 10

84 CALORIES PER SERVING: 3 G PROTEIN, 0 G FAT, 17 G CARBOHYDRATE; 335 MG SODIUM; 0 MG CHOLESTEROL

Curried Squash Soup

Bright golden-orange in color, and sweet and spicy in flavor. I serve this soup with bowls of raisins, sliced apples, and yogurt on the side.

1 large	butternut squash, peeled, seeded, and cut into large chunks (about 2½ to 3 pounds)
1	all-purpose potato, peeled and cut into cubes
1	tart apple, peeled, cored, and quartered
1	leek, washed well and chopped
1 large clove	garlic, peeled and crushed
1 teaspoon	minced fresh ginger
1 tablespoon	vegetable oil
¼ teaspoon	ground cardamom
1 teaspoon	ground coriander
¼ teaspoon	ground turmeric
2 teaspoons	curry powder
2 teaspoons	soy sauce
⅟₁₆ to ⅛ teaspoon	cayenne pepper
	raisins and sliced apple for garnish

1. Put the squash, potato, and apple into a pot, add enough water to cover by 1 inch, and bring to a boil. Reduce to a simmer and cook, uncovered, until the squash is tender, about 20 minutes.
2. Sauté the leek, garlic, and ginger in the oil. Add to the boiled vegetables and stir in the spices and seasonings.
3. Puree mixture, then return to the pot. Simmer for 10 minutes longer.
4. Taste and adjust the seasonings, and serve garnished with raisins and sliced apples.

Serves 8

111 CALORIES PER SERVING: 2 G PROTEIN, 2 G FAT, 24 G CARBOHYDRATE; 94 MG SODIUM; 0 MG CHOLESTEROL

Minestrone

Don't be deterred by this long list of ingredients. Minestrone is easy to make and an all-time favorite.

½	Spanish onion, chopped
2 ribs	celery, chopped
2 tablespoons	olive oil
2 cloves	garlic, minced
28-ounce can	whole tomatoes
½ cup	chopped green cabbage
1	carrot, chopped
1	zucchini, chopped
2 tablespoons	minced fresh parsley
2 cups	water or stock
4 cups	tomato juice
⅔ cup	cooked chick-peas (or any leftover bean or pasta)
1	bay leaf
1 tablespoon	dried basil
1 teaspoon	dried oregano
½ teaspoon	dried thyme
	freshly ground pepper to taste

1. Sauté the onion and celery in the olive oil. Cover and cook on low heat for 15 minutes. If more cooking liquid is needed, add some tomato juice from the canned tomatoes.
2. Add the garlic and cook for 5 more minutes.
3. Crush the tomatoes with your hands as you add them and the juice from the can to the sautéed vegetables.
4. Stir in the remaining ingredients and simmer, uncovered, for 45 minutes.
5. If the soup is too thick, thin with water or tomato juice.

Serves 9

98 CALORIES PER SERVING: 3 G PROTEIN, 4 G FAT, 15 G CARBOHYDRATE;
548 MG SODIUM; 0 MG CHOLESTEROL

Quinoa Vegetable Soup

This soup takes only half an hour to cook because quinoa is such a fast-cooking grain. The result is a light but filling soup with vegetables that are fresh-tasting, not boiled. If quinoa is not available, use precooked pasta or rice instead and reduce the water by 1 cup.

1 clove	garlic, minced
1	carrot, diced
½	yellow onion, diced
¼	green bell pepper, chopped
½ cup	chopped green cabbage
1 tablespoon	vegetable or olive oil
¼ cup	quinoa, rinsed
3 cups	water or stock
1 cup	corn kernels
14-ounce can	whole tomatoes
¼ cup	chopped fresh parsley
¼ teaspoon	dried thyme
1	bay leaf
½ teaspoon	salt
	freshly ground pepper to taste

1. Sauté the garlic, carrot, onion, bell pepper, and cabbage in the oil over low heat until the onion becomes translucent.
2. Add the quinoa and cook until the quinoa grains begin to pop. Add the water, corn, tomatoes, herbs, and seasonings. (Crush the tomatoes before dropping them into the pot.)
3. Simmer for 30 minutes and serve immediately

Serves 6

106 CALORIES PER SERVING: 3 G PROTEIN, 3 G FAT, 19 G CARBOHYDRATE; 296 MG SODIUM; 0 MG CHOLESTEROL

ENTRÉES

Chicken Dishes

◆

As everyone is by now aware, poultry is a protein source that nutritionists love. Leave off the skin, and you cut its already moderate fat
calories in half; eat only the white meat and the cholesterol is very
low. It is true that white, skinless poultry meat is boring on its own,
but using herbs and spices and browning the meat bring out more
flavor. With this in mind, I created the following recipes solely with
white meat chicken. They are flavorful, simple, and attractive, but
low in fat and cholesterol.

Chicken Baked in Mustard

This is an embarrassingly simple recipe that I learned while a brunch
chef at a French restaurant. It is my stand-by fast dinner, and leftovers
are great in sandwiches. I keep it interesting by using different special-
ty mustards. My current favorite is a hot horseradish brown mustard
made in Vermont.

2	whole skinless, boneless chicken breasts (about 1 to 1½ pounds total)
¼ cup	good-quality prepared mustard
½ to 1 cup	bread crumbs, preferably soft, whole wheat, and homemade

1. Cut the chicken into 4 equal pieces and pat dry with a paper towel.
2. Brush the mustard onto both sides of the chicken, roll each piece in
   the bread crumbs, coating thoroughly, and gently shake off the
   excess.
3. Bake in a preheated 400 degree F oven for 20 minutes or until
   done.

Serves 4

182 CALORIES PER SERVING: 25 G PROTEIN, 4 G FAT, 10 G CARBOHYDRATE;
351 MG SODIUM; 61 MG CHOLESTEROL

Balsamic Chicken and Broccoli

If asparagus is in season, feel free to use it as a substitute. Fresh green beans also work nicely.

1 tablespoon	olive oil
1 to 2 cloves	garlic, minced
½ small	yellow onion, thinly sliced, then cut slices into thirds
2 tablespoons	minced shallots
¼ cup	white wine
2	whole skinless, boneless chicken breasts, cut into strips (about 1 to 1½ pounds total)
3 tablespoons	balsamic vinegar
2 cups	broccoli spears (a good use for leftover lightly steamed ones)
1 cup	mushrooms (preferably fancy ones like oyster or shiitake), sliced or left whole, depending on the type used
⅓ cup	chicken stock
¼ teaspoon	salt
	pasta or brown rice
	freshly ground pepper to taste

1. Heat the oil in a heavy pot. Add the garlic, onion, and shallots and cook until light golden. Keep the pot covered between stirrings and use a tablespoon or so of the wine if more liquid is needed.
2. Add the strips of chicken and enough of the wine to keep the meat from sticking to the pot. Cook until the chicken is white all the way through, about 5 to 7 minutes (use more wine, if needed).
3. Remove the chicken and sautéed vegetables with a slotted spoon.
4. Add the vinegar to the pot, increase the heat, and stir with a wooden spoon, scraping bits from the bottom, until the liquid is reduced to about half its volume and is thickened.
5. Reduce the heat. Return the chicken and sautéed vegetables to the pot, add the broccoli, mushrooms, stock, remaining wine, and salt. Cook at a gentle simmer until the broccoli turns bright green.
6. Serve over pasta or brown rice, and dust with pepper.

Serves 4

201 CALORIES PER SERVING: 25 G PROTEIN, 6 G FAT, 9 G CARBOHYDRATE; 206 MG SODIUM; 61 MG CHOLESTEROL

Fragrant Chicken

This recipe, with its Spanish overtones, is both fragrant and visually appealing. Although it calls for more ingredients and takes a little more time to prepare than most of my other recipes, it is not difficult to make. If baked in an attractive casserole dish, it can go straight from the stove top to the dining room table.

2	whole skinless, boneless chicken breasts (about 1½ pounds total)
1 teaspoon	freshly ground pepper
½	teaspoon ground cinnamon
⅛ teaspoon	ground cloves
¼ teaspoon	salt
½ teaspoon	ground turmeric
¼ cup	unbleached white flour
1 tablespoon	olive oil
½ to 1 cup	white wine or chicken stock
2 cloves	garlic, minced
⅓ cup	chopped yellow onion
1 cup	orange juice
pinch	saffron
3 tablespoons	seedless golden raisins
1 tablespoon	capers
¼ teaspoon	salt
1	orange, peeled to remove the white pith, and sliced

1. Cut the chicken into 3- to 4-ounce pieces.
2. Combine the spices and the flour in a plastic bag. Add the chicken, one piece at a time, and shake until well coated.
3. Heat the oil and some of the wine in a large skillet. Add the chicken and cook until the meat turns white on all sides. Do not crowd the pieces of chicken.
4. Remove the chicken from the skillet and add the remaining wine, garlic, and onion. Sauté until the vegetables are soft. With a wooden spoon, scrape the flour from the bottom of the skillet, stirring constantly. The flour will form a light gravy later.
5. Return the chicken to the skillet and add the remaining ingredients, except for the orange slices. If necessary, add a little stock so the sauce comes halfway up the chicken. Cover and simmer for 30 minutes.

6. Add the orange slices, cook for 5 minutes longer, and serve immediately.

Serves 4

322 CALORIES PER SERVING: 36 G PROTEIN, 8 G FAT, 25 G CARBOHYDRATE; 399 MG SODIUM; 92 MG CHOLESTEROL

Marmalade Chicken

Preparation time is minimal. Success is guaranteed.

4	whole skinless chicken breasts, with bones (about 2 to 3 pounds total)
¼ cup	unbleached white flour
2 teaspoons	olive oil
¼ cup	chicken stock
½ teaspoon	dried marjoram
½ teaspoon	grated lemon zest
2 tablespoons	sherry
1 teaspoon	soy sauce
¼ cup	orange marmalade (preferably sweetened with honey)
1	orange

1. Dust the chicken with the flour. Heat a small amount of olive oil in a skillet and lightly brown the chicken. When done, place in a single layer in a casserole dish.
2. Combine the stock, marjoram, lemon zest, sherry, and soy sauce. Pour over the chicken, then brush the chicken with marmalade.
3. Using a sharp paring knife, peel the orange, removing the white pith along with the peel. Cut the segments away from the membranes. Do this over the casserole dish, which will catch the fresh juice as you work. Arrange the orange segments over the chicken.
4. Bake in a preheated 375 degree F oven for 30–40 minutes.

Serves 8

184 CALORIES PER SERVING: 23 G PROTEIN, 4 G FAT, 12 G CARBOHYDRATE; 98 MG SODIUM; 61 MG CHOLESTEROL

Country Chicken

For casual dinner parties, for midweek family meals, or as a dish that can be frozen and reheated after a long day at work, this recipe never fails. And, it doesn't use any oil. Give it a try and it might become a standard in your repertoire.

2	whole chicken breasts, with bones, skinned and quartered (about 1½ to 2 pounds total)
	unbleached white flour
3 cups	chicken stock
2 cloves	garlic, minced
6	small white onions, peeled (also called pearl onions)
10	large mushrooms, wiped clean and quartered
1½ cups	whole canned tomatoes, including the juice
1 teaspoon	dried thyme
¼ cup	minced fresh parsley
2	bay leaves
1 tablespoon	soy sauce
	freshly ground pepper to taste

1. Lightly dust the chicken with the flour. Heat a thin layer of stock in a heavy pot. Brown the chicken, adding more stock as necessary. Once browned, remove the chicken to a plate.
2. In the same pot, sauté the garlic and onions in the remaining stock. Scrape up the flour from the bottom of the pan with a wooden spoon. This will form a gravy with the next ingredients.
3. Add the mushrooms and sauté for a few minutes until they wilt. Add the tomatoes, breaking them apart with your hands as they go into the pot. Return the chicken to the pot, add the remaining ingredients, and simmer, covered, for 30 minutes.

Serves 4

206 CALORIES PER SERVING: 32 G PROTEIN, 4 G FAT, 10 G CARBOHYDRATE; 479 MG SODIUM; 82 MG CHOLESTEROL

Sunburst Salad, page 41

Dressed Asparagus, page 33

elon-Berry Swirl, page 60

Mussels in a Shallot Sauce, page 101

emon Rosemary Chicken, page 90

The Squeeze, page 97

Four Peppers and Salmon Over Pasta, page 99

Oriental Chicken in Parchment, page 91

Chinese Dumpling Rolls, page 120

ean Enchiladas, page 109

Current Currant Carrot Cake, page 156, with "Marshmallow Fluff," page 157

Oatmeal Drop Cookies, page 163; Almond Loves, page 166; Jam Squares, page 161

More Than Apple Pie, page 171

ssorted Muffins, pages 174-178

Poached Pears in Raspberry Sauce, page 150

Apple Cider Chicken

This dish is like a stew, and is especially good ladled over rice or pasta.

¼ cup	unbleached white flour
½ teaspoon	salt
¼ teaspoon	freshly ground pepper
2	whole, skinless, boneless chicken breasts, cut into cubes (about 1 to 1½ pounds total)
4 teaspoons	corn oil (less if a nonstick pan is used)
1	yellow onion, cut in half and thinly sliced, then cut in half once more
2	fresh tomatoes, chopped, or 14-ounce can, drained
1 cup	apple cider
1 tablespoon	chopped fresh basil, or 1 teaspoon dried
1	teaspoon grated orange peel (avoid the white pith underneath the skin)

1. Combine the flour, salt, and pepper in a plastic bag.
2. Shake the chicken, a few pieces at a time, in the flour until lightly coated.
3. Heat the oil in a heavy pot and add the chicken. Cook until flesh is white on all sides. (You might have to do this in several batches, so you don't crowd the chicken.)
4. Remove the chicken from the pot and set aside. Sauté the onion in the pot. If needed, add a little cider or some stock.
5. Add the tomatoes and apple cider to the pot, along with the chicken. Simmer gently, covered, for 20 minutes.
6. Add the basil and orange peel, cook for 10 more minutes, and serve.

Serves 4

206 CALORIES PER SERVING: 24 G PROTEIN, 4 G FAT, 18 G CARBOHYDRATE; 330 MG SODIUM; 61 MG CHOLESTEROL

An Herbal Composition

Fresh herbs are a must! If you can't find some of the ones listed here, substitute others, such as tarragon, sage, and oregano.

1 cup	white wine
1 tablespoon	olive oil
1 clove	garlic, crushed
2	bay leaves
6	green peppercorns, crushed
¼ teaspoon	salt
1 teapoon	chopped fresh thyme
2 teaspoons	chopped fresh rosemary
2 tablespoons	chopped fresh basil
2 to 3	whole skinless, boneless chicken breasts (about 2 to 2½ pounds total)

1. Combine all of the ingredients, except chicken, in a nonreactive dish and let sit at room temperature for at least an hour.
2. Add the chicken breasts and marinate, refrigerated, for 1 hour, then broil or grill until done. Chicken cooks quickly (in about 10 minutes) over high heat. Turn once. Baste with marinade while cooking to keep the meat from drying out.

Serves 6

207 CALORIES PER SERVING: 30 G PROTEIN, 6 G FAT, 1 G CARBOHYDRATE; 184 MG SODIUM; 82 MG CHOLESTEROL

Chicken in a Chili Tomato Sauce

This sauce is good for baking fish as well as chicken. Use about 1 cup for each pound of meat, and freeze the excess, if you like, for another time. (This recipe makes about 5 cups sauce.)

2 teaspoons	vegetable or olive oil
1	small onion, chopped
6 ribs	celery, chopped
½	green bell pepper, chopped
¼ cup	white wine
3 cups	peeled, seeded tomatoes (canned or fresh, see page 63)
½ tablespoon	soy sauce
1 teaspoon	chili powder, or to taste
2 tablespoons	lemon juice
2 cloves	garlic, chopped
⅛ teaspoon	red pepper flakes
¼ cup	tomato juice
dash	hot pepper sauce
2	whole skinless, boneless chicken breasts (about 1 to 1½ pounds total)

1. Heat the oil in a pot and sauté the onion, celery, and bell pepper. As more liquid is needed, add the wine.
2. Stir in the remaining ingredients, except chicken, cover, and simmer for 15 minutes.
3. Cool slightly, then puree.
4. Place chicken in a baking dish, cover with 1 to 1½ cups sauce, and bake in a preheated 375 degree F oven for 20–30 minutes.

Serves 4

137 CALORIES PER SERVING: 23 G PROTEIN, 3 G FAT, 3 G CARBOHYDRATE; 108 MG SODIUM; 61 MG CHOLESTEROL

Chicken with Indonesian Sauce

Another favorite use for this sauce is as a marinade for squares of tofu, which can then be baked to a crisp, and used as filling for pita pocket sandwiches.

1½ tablespoons	lime juice
2 tablespoons	chunky unsalted peanut butter
2 teaspoons	soy sauce
1 tablespoon	good-quality prepared mustard
1 tablespoon	honey
1½ tablespoons	water
¼ teaspoon	hot pepper sauce
pinch	ground hot chili pepper (optional)
2	whole skinless, boneless chicken breasts, cut into strips (about 1 to 1½ pounds total)
	sesame oil

1. Puree all ingredients but the chicken and sesame oil.
2. Place chicken in a nonreactive dish, pour on sauce, and marinate, refrigerated, for at least 30 minutes.
3. Heat a small amount of sesame oil in a wok, add chicken pieces, and stir-fry until cooked through. If you want to accompany this with leftover marinade, be sure to heat the marinade thoroughly before serving.

Serves 4

189 CALORIES PER SERVING: 25 G PROTEIN, 7 G FAT, 6 G CARBOHYDRATE; 279 MG SODIUM; 61 MG CHOLESTEROL

Southern Chicken Stew

A friend's husband calls this his favorite vegetarian (!) dish, and requests it often. Even with the potatoes, corn, and lima beans, it is lighter than a beef stew, yet just as satisfying.

1 pound	red bliss potatoes, scrubbed, then cut into ½-inch cubes
2 cups	canned tomatoes, including the juice
1	yellow onion, chopped
1 cup	chicken stock
½ cup	lima beans, frozen, not dried
1 cup	corn kernels
2	whole skinless, boneless chicken breasts, cut into large chunks (about 1 to 1½ pounds total)
1 tablespoon	molasses
½ teaspoon	salt
¼ teaspoon	freshly ground pepper
⅛ teaspoon	cayenne pepper
1 tablespoon	tomato paste (optional)

1. Cook the potatoes, tomatoes, and onion in the stock until the potatoes start to soften, about 7 minutes.
2. Add the lima beans, corn, and chicken, and cook until the chicken turns white all the way through, about 12 minutes.
3. Add the remaining ingredients and simmer for at least 20 minutes. (Like all stews, this will taste best if it is allowed a long, slow cooking time and is served the next day. If you do want to eat it right away, thicken it with a tablespoon of tomato paste.)

Serves 4

317 CALORIES PER SERVING: 29 G PROTEIN, 3 G FAT, 45 G CARBOHYDRATE; 567 MG SODIUM; 61 MG CHOLESTEROL

Sesame Buttermilk Chicken

For best results, bake chicken in a heavy, dark casserole dish. Clear glass dries it out and thin tin cooks it unevenly. Garnish this with color in mind. Use paprika, minced parsley, thin strips of roasted red pepper, or whatever else seems appropriate.

4	whole skinless, boneless chicken breasts (about 2 to 3 pounds total)
½ teaspoon	freshly ground pepper
⅓ cup	sesame seeds, toasted
½ cup	bread crumbs
1 cup	buttermilk (this amount will vary depending on the size of the baking dish)

1. Cut the chicken into 8 pieces (about 4 ounces each). Pat dry, then rub on the pepper.
2. Mix together the sesame seeds and bread crumbs. Dip the chicken in buttermilk and roll in the crumb mixture, coating well.
3. Place the chicken in a casserole dish and pour in enough buttermilk to reach halfway up the chicken. Top the chicken with the remaining bread crumbs.
4. Cover and bake in a preheated 375 degrees F oven for 20 minutes. Uncover and bake for 10 minutes longer. Serve with a colorful garnish.

Serves 8

188 CALORIES PER SERVING: 27 G PROTEIN, 6 G FAT, 6 G CARBOHYDRATE; 134 MG SODIUM; 62 MG CHOLESTEROL

Bread Crumbs

Because commercially produced bread crumbs usually contain bleached white flour, hydrogenated vegetable oil, and artificial flavorings, I make my own. Any whole wheat bread is suitable as long as it is not strongly flavored and has no seeds. Use stale but not moldy bread, or dry out fresh slices in a warm oven. Break the bread into pieces, put in a food processor fitted with metal blade, and process until crumbs have the desired texture. Bread crumbs stored in a tightly closed container last for a month in the cupboard, 6 months in the freezer.

Honey Teriyaki Chicken

This versatile dish is also good with stir-fried vegetables.

¼ cup	soy sauce
1 tablespoon	minced fresh ginger
1 clove	garlic, minced
½ cup	water
1 tablespoon	lemon juice
1½ tablespoons	honey
6	scallions, sliced
2	whole skinless, boneless chicken breasts, cut into thin strips (about 1 to 1½ pounds total)

1. Whisk together all ingredients except the chicken. Mix with chicken in nonreactive dish and marinate for 30 minutes.
2. Heat a wok and add a thin layer of the marinade. Sauté the chicken in this liquid until the pieces are cooked through, about 7 minutes. Stir in the rest of the marinade, cover, and cook 5 minutes longer. (Add vegetables at this point, if using them.)

Serves 4, more if vegetables are added

164 CALORIES PER SERVING: 24 G PROTEIN, 3 G FAT, 10 G CARBOHYDRATE; 825 MG SODIUM; 61 MG CHOLESTEROL

Lemon Thyme Chicken Rolls

As with the Lemon Rosemary Chicken recipe (see page 90), this also uses a lemony marinade that makes the chicken breasts exceptionally moist and tender. If you can find fancy fresh oyster or shiitake mushrooms, use them instead of, or in addition to, the regular mushrooms.

2	whole skinless, boneless chicken breasts (about 1 to 1½ pounds total)
¼ cup	lemon juice
¼ cup	white wine plus 1 to 2 teaspoons
2 cloves	garlic, peeled and crushed
1 teaspoon	dried thyme
2 teaspoons	olive oil
1	shallot, minced
2¼ cups	sliced mushrooms (about ¼ pound)
1½ tablespoons	minced fresh parsley
⅛ teaspoon	salt
⅛ teaspoon	freshly ground pepper

1. Trim the chicken of any fat. Cut each whole breast into 2 portions, removing the cartilage. If there are tenderloins (those fingerlike pieces of meat on the inside of the breast), remove them and save for another purpose.
2. With a smooth meat mallet or other similar tool, pound the breasts until they are a uniform thickness, preferably about ¼ inch. Pieces that start out thin still need to be pounded, but not energetically. A very thick breast may need to be sliced in half horizontally.
3. Whisk together the lemon juice, ¼ cup wine, garlic, and thyme. Pour over chicken and marinate for 2-8 hours, refrigerated.
4. Just before chicken has finished marinating, heat the oil in a pan. Sauté the shallot until soft. Add 2 cups of the mushrooms, 1 to 2 teaspoons wine, parsley, salt, and pepper. Cook gently until the mushrooms soften and shrink in size.
5. Remove the chicken from the marinade onto a clean surface. Place a portion of mushrooms in the center of each piece of chicken. Starting at the narrower end, tightly roll up the chicken and arrange in a casserole, seam side down, so the rolls are close but not touching.
6. Strain the marinade over the chicken.
7. Cover and bake in a preheated 350 degree F oven for 20 minutes.
8. Place the cooked chicken on a serving plate and keep warm. Pour

the baking liquid into a small saucepan, add the remaining ¼ cup of mushrooms and boil until the liquid cooks down to only a few tablespoons. Pour over the chicken and serve.

Serves 4

169 CALORIES PER SERVING: 24 G PROTEIN, 5 G FAT, 4 G CARBOHYDRATE; 133 MG SODIUM; 61 MG CHOLESTEROL

Chicken in Orange and Tahini

As a variation, cut the chicken into bite-sized pieces and serve on toothpicks as an hors d'oeuvre.

1 clove	garlic, peeled and crushed
¾ cup	orange juice
1 tablespoon	frozen orange juice concentrate
1 tablespoon	soy sauce
2 tablespoons	tahini
2	whole skinless, boneless chicken breasts, cut into 3- to 4-ounce portions (about 1 pound total)
1 tablespoon	sesame seeds

1. Combine the garlic, ½ cup of the orange juice, orange juice concentrate, soy sauce, and tahini, blending well. Marinate the chicken in this mixture for 1 hour in the refrigerator.
2. Remove the chicken from the marinade and place in a baking dish.
3. Pour the remaining ¼ cup orange juice over the chicken and add as much of the marinade as is necessary to cover ¾ of the chicken.
4. Sprinkle the sesame seeds on top.
5. Bake in a preheated 375 degree F oven for 30 minutes.

Serves 4

206 CALORIES PER SERVING: 25 G PROTEIN, 8 G FAT, 9 G CARBOHYDRATE; 321 MG SODIUM; 61 MG CHOLESTEROL

Lemon Rosemary Chicken

Marinating chicken breasts in lemon juice produces the most tender, succulent meat imaginable. Hot or cold, this is excellent.

2	whole skinless chicken breasts, with bones (about 1½ to 2 pounds total)
2	lemons
¼ cup	unbleached white flour
½ teaspoon	paprika
¼ teaspoon	salt
¼ teaspoon	freshly ground pepper
½ cup	chicken stock
1 teaspoon	malt syrup
1 tablespoon	chopped fresh rosemary, or 1 teaspoon crushed dried

1. Halve the chicken breasts and put into a glass or stainless steel bowl.
2. Juice the lemons, strain to remove seeds, and pour the juice over the chicken. Cover with plastic wrap and store in the refrigerator for a minimum of 4 hours, and a maximum of 12.
3. Remove the chicken from the bowl and discard the lemon juice.
4. Put the flour, paprika, salt, and pepper in a plastic bag and shake to mix. Add chicken, one piece at a time, and shake until well coated with flour.
5. Place chicken in a baking pan or oven-proof casserole and bake in a preheated 375 degree F oven for 20 minutes.
6. Remove the baking pan from the oven, pour in the combined chicken stock, malt syrup, and rosemary, and return to the oven. Bake for another 15 minutes.
7. If a sauce is desired, place the chicken on a warm plate, put the baking pan with juices on the stove top, and boil at a high heat for about 4 minutes, stirring frequently, until the volume is reduced by half. Pour over the chicken and serve.

Serves 4

159 CALORIES PER SERVING: 23 G PROTEIN, 3 G FAT, 9 G CARBOHYDRATE; 188 MG SODIUM; 61 MG CHOLESTEROL

Oriental Chicken in Parchment

There is an air of anticipation when opening these surprise packages as their aroma is released and their contents revealed. This recipe makes two packets, each about 4 ounces. If you want to expand the recipe, the marinade can be doubled or tripled.

½ teaspoon	toasted sesame oil
1 clove	garlic, crushed
1 slice	fresh ginger, minced
1 teaspoon	soy sauce
2 tablespoons	sherry
1	whole skinless, boneless chicken breast, cut in half along the cartilage (about ½ to ¾ pound total)
2 tablespoons	julienned leeks
½	carrot, cut into matchsticks
6 slices	julienned red bell pepper
2 slices	fresh ginger, peeled

1. Combine the toasted sesame oil, garlic, minced ginger, soy sauce, and sherry. Pour over the chicken, cover, and refrigerate for at least 2 hours.
2. Cut 2 pieces of parchment paper, each slightly more than double the size of the chicken. Fold the sheets of parchment in half.
3. Divide the ingredients into two equal portions and arrange as follows for both packets: first, put the leeks on one side of the folded parchment, then place the carrots on top of the leeks, followed by the chicken. Crisscross the bell pepper over the chicken, and place the ginger next to the chicken. Fold the other half of the parchment paper over the chicken, and with a knife edge, crease and seal the ends of the packets.
4. Place the closed packets on a baking dish and bake in a preheated 350 degrees F oven for 30 minutes.
5. Remove packets from the oven and place on dinner plates. Being careful of the escaping steam, cut an X in both and serve.

Serves 2

184 CALORIES PER SERVING: 24 G PROTEIN, 4 G FAT, 9 G CARBOHYDRATE;
238 MG SODIUM; 61 MG CHOLESTEROL

Cooking with Parchment Paper

Cooking chicken, fish, or vegetables in a parchment-paper packet is a traditional technique called "en papillote," which translated from the French means "cooking in a cocoon."

When food is prepared in this manner, steam is trapped inside, which both cooks the food and keeps it moist. The packet puffs out from the steam, but enough moisture escapes through the paper's pores so that it doesn't burst open. Although this resembles cooking in foil packets, it is not the same. Because steam can't escape from foil, both the texture and the flavor of the food are adversely affected. Also, foil insulates, requiring a longer cooking time. In addition, acidic ingredients eat away at foil and might leave flakes of metal in the food.

Gentle cooking with parchment paper is perfect for delicate fish fillets and chicken breasts. Because the packet retains all of the food's juices, flavors intensify. Although traditionally *en papillote* called for butter and heavy sauces, low-fat recipes are ideally suited to this cooking technique. A little olive oil or lemon juice is all the moisture that needs to be added.

Fish and Shellfish

Nutritionists suggest that people eat more fish, especially the fatty fishes, although the lean ones are good for you, too. All are a low-calorie, low-fat source of protein.

Shellfish are also low in fat, and the mollusks (clams and mussels) are especially low in cholesterol as well. The crustaceans (shrimp and lobster) have about the same cholesterol levels as meat, but they are so low in saturated fat that they are still a smart food choice.

There are other reasons for buying seafood. Today's selection of fish is larger and fresher than ever. Sure, you can stick with the familiar cod and sole, but you can also get monkfish, mako shark, catfish, and mahi-mahi. The lesser-known varieties are often good buys, plus they taste great and are easy to cook.

Fish can be divided into two basic categories regarding flavor and cooking methods. The dark, oily, firm fishes are best broiled, baked, or grilled. The white, more delicate varieties are better steamed, poached, or baked in liquid. Within each category, fish can be interchanged. For example, tuna, halibut steaks, swordfish, and shark can generally be cooked the same way.

Buying Fish and Shellfish

You have heard this before but it is worth repeating: buy only the freshest fish. Those caught in the ocean should smell slightly of salt water and seaweed, and those from fresh water should smell clean. Fish should never have a strong "fishy" smell. The flesh should feel firm when pressed with a finger. Look for whole fish with pink gills and bulging, watery eyes, or fillets that are a uniform color and have no trace of sliminess.

Whole fish must have their viscera removed immediately. Store fish on ice in the refrigerator for no longer than two days, and never keep it wrapped tightly in plastic. Mollusks must be live when purchased. If they don't clamp shut when tapped, throw them out. They can be stored in the refrigerator, covered with a damp towel, for up to four days.

How to Tell When the Fish Is Done

What does it mean when a cookbook tells you to cook the fish until it "flakes?" Look at a piece of raw fish and notice how the muscles are striated in one direction. Try gently prying the fish apart along the lines of the muscles with a fork. An uncooked fish will stay together. In a partially cooked fish the fork will go in part way. The fish is done when a fork can, with almost no effort, go all the way through the fillet and form flakes of the flesh.

Color is another indication of whether the fish is cooked. A white-fleshed fish will change from a cloudy, bluish white to a brighter white. When cooked, the white color will extend throughout the fish. A dark-fleshed fish will also change color. The pink tone of the flesh on the inside will become more like the color on the out-side as it cooks.

Fish is often overcooked, which ruins both the texture and the flavor. Thin fillets cook in under 7 minutes, and they flake easily. It is more difficult to judge when a thick fillet is done. They can take up to 20 minutes to cook. If the outside of the fish starts to dry out before the inside flakes, a little cooking liquid may be added or a cover put over the pan. The inside of a thick fillet will not flake apart, but it will firm up and the color will change. Because fish cooks in such a short time, it requires close attention. If in doubt, slightly undercook the fish; retained heat will finish the job.

If the thickness of a fish varies significantly, remove the thinner section when it is done and finish cooking the remainder. Or before cooking, fold the thin section over onto itself, so that it is about as thick as the rest of the fish.

Poached Fish

This simplest approach to fish cookery has several benefits: It is fast, it is next to impossible to overcook, there is little clean-up, and there are no lingering fish odors in the kitchen.

2 parts	white wine
1 part	lemon juice
1 pound	fish fillet
	herbs of your choice

1. Bring the wine and lemon juice to a simmer in a pan with a lid. The amount of poaching liquid depends on the thickness of the fish and the size of the pan. The liquid should cover ¾ of the fish.
2. Place the fish fillet(s) in the pan and add your choice of herbs. Those usually associated with seafood include dill, thyme, and chervil.
3. Cover and gently simmer until the fish flakes. Thin fillets, such as flounder, take less than 5 minutes; thicker ones, such as haddock, take from 7–10.

Serves 4

77 CALORIES PER SERVING: 17 G PROTEIN, 1 G FAT, 0 G CARBOHYDRATE; 64 MG SODIUM; 0 MG CHOLESTEROL (analysis based on sole)

Baked Fish in Almost Sour Cream

I didn't start cooking until college but even then, most nights I ate spaghetti or fish sticks. Then I discovered the *Joy of Cooking* and learned that I was capable of making much more. Fish baked in sour cream was so simple that it replaced frozen fish sticks in my repertoire. I've since revamped that recipe, adding new ingredients and removing the fat, but my version retains the same ease as the original.

1 pound	fish fillet, preferably a thick, flavorful variety such as haddock, hake, or perch
	juice from 1 lemon (about ¼ cup)
1 cup	Almost Sour Cream (see page 185)
1 tablespoon	minced fresh chives, dill, or tarragon (optional)
	freshly ground pepper

1. Place the fish, skin side down, in a baking dish. Squeeze the lemon over the fish.
2. Combine the Almost Sour Cream with chives, dill, or tarragon, if desired, and spread on top of the fish.
3. Cover and bake in a preheated 375 degree F oven for 15–20 minutes (less time with thin fish). Uncover and bake for 5 minutes longer.
4. Grind pepper over the fillet and serve.

Serves 4

148 CALORIES PER SERVING: 29 G PROTEIN, 2 G FAT, 3 G CARBOHYDRATE; 286 MG SODIUM; 69 MG CHOLESTEROL (analysis based on haddock)

Ginger and Lime Fish

So much flavor with so little fuss—an ideal entrée for company.

1 pound	thick fish fillet (such as cod or halibut)
2 teaspoons	minced fresh ginger
1 tablespoon	soy sauce
3	limes, juiced (about ¼ to ⅓ cup)
2 tablespoons	water (if necessary)
	lime slices for garnish

1. Place the fillet skin side down in a baking dish.
2. Combine the ginger, soy sauce, and lime juice. Pour over the fish. Add water if there isn't ¼ inch of liquid covering the bottom of the pan. (If time permits, marinate for 30 minutes.)
3. Bake in a preheated 375 degrees F oven for 20–25 minutes, or until fish flakes easily.
4. Serve garnished with lime slices.

Serves 4

132 CALORIES PER SERVING: 24 G PROTEIN, 3 G FAT, 2 G CARBOHYDRATE; 319 MG SODIUM; 36 MG CHOLESTEROL

Garlic Broiled Fish

Serve the marinade as a sauce and accompany with crusty bread to soak up all the flavorful juices.

3 tablespoons	lemon juice
3 tablespoons	olive oil
2 cloves	garlic, peeled and crushed
1	shallot, peeled and crushed
¼ teaspoon	hot pepper sauce
2 teaspoons	chopped fresh parsley
1 to 1½ pounds	fish fillet, preferably thick

1. Combine the lemon juice, olive oil, and seasonings in a bowl. Marinate the fish in this mixture, refrigerated, for at least 1 hour, or as long as 6. (Marinate thin, mild-flavored fish for no longer than 30 minutes.)

2. Place the fish, skin side down, in a baking pan. Pour the marinade around the fillet and add enough water to cover ⅔ of the fish.
3. Broil the fish until it flakes easily with a fork, then serve immediately.

Serves 4

128 CALORIES PER SERVING: 28 G PROTEIN, 12 G FAT, 2 G CARBOHYDRATE; 121 MG SODIUM; 77 MG CHOLESTEROL (analysis based on sole)

The Squeeze

A great marinade for firm-fleshed fish, such as tuna, swordfish, or mahi-mahi. Also perfect for chicken. Be sure to use only freshly squeezed juice.

¼ cup	lime juice (1 or 2 limes)
⅓ cup	pink grapefruit juice (½ grapefruit)
½ cup	orange juice (2 juice oranges)
½ tablespoon	olive oil
¼ teaspoon	soy sauce
½ tablespoon	grated fresh ginger
2 cloves	garlic, peeled and crushed
1	shallot, peeled and quartered
⅛ teaspoon	hot pepper sauce
1 pound	thick fish fillets or steaks of your choice

1. Whisk together all but last ingredient and let rest at least 1 hour.
2. Place fish in marinade and refrigerate for 1 hour, turning from time to time.
3. Transfer fish to oven-proof dish, pour marinade around it to a depth of ¼ inch, then place under the broiler. Cook until fish flakes easily.

Serves 4

183 CALORIES PER SERVING: 23 G PROTEIN, 6 G FAT, 8 G CARBOHYDRATE; 168 MG SODIUM; 44 MG CHOLESTEROL (analysis based on swordfish)

Fish with Mustard and Apples

I make this with salmon; the pinkish fish under a blanket of apples, surrounded by a piquant mustard sauce is an impressive sight. But the charm of this dish doesn't stop there—it's also a snap to prepare.

1 tablespoon	minced shallot
1 teaspoon	oil
1 pound	fish fillet (such as salmon or perch)
1	tart, firm apple
1 teaspoon	lemon juice
3 tablespoons	pommery or other coarse mustard
¼ cup	white wine
3 tablespoons	water or fish stock (some gourmet stores carry dehydrated low-salt fish stock)

1. Sauté the shallots in the oil until softened. Leaving the oil in the pan, remove the shallots with a slotted spoon and transfer them to the bottom of a casserole dish; then place the fish on top.
2. Core and thinly slice the apple. Sauté in the remaining oil with the lemon juice until it softens but is not mushy. Toss or turn the slices several times during cooking.
3. Arrange the apple slices on top of the fish. I like to overlap them so they look like scales. (You may not need all of the apple.)
4. Whisk together the mustard, wine, and water, and pour over and around the fish, adding more water until it reaches halfway up the side of the fillet.
5. Bake in a preheated 375 degree F oven until the fish is done (about 8–10 minutes for the average fillet).
6. If a sauce is desired, remove the fish to a serving platter (a spatula is the best tool for this), then strain the liquid through a sieve and into a saucepan. Boil it, stirring constantly, until it is reduced to about 3 tablespoons and is a thick consistency. Pour over the fish and serve.

Serves 4

156 CALORIES PER SERVING: 23 G PROTEIN, 3 G FAT, 7 G CARBOHYDRATE; 233 MG SODIUM; 102 MG CHOLESTEROL (analysis based on perch)

Four Peppers and Salmon Over Pasta

Bell peppers, beautifully cut, can transform a dish from average to elegant. Also, uniformly julienned peppers will cook quickly and evenly. Part of the pleasure of this dish derives from its lovely appearance when all of the colors and shapes are brought together at the end.

¼ pound	pasta (rotini or a short, nubby variety)
1	red bell pepper
1	green bell pepper
1 clove	garlic, chopped
1 tablespoon	corn oil
1 tablespoon	olive oil
½ pound	fresh poached salmon, flaked (or water-packed salmon, bones and skin removed)
1 tablespoon	green peppercorns packed in water or vinegar (not dried)
⅛ teaspoon	salt
¼ teaspoon	freshly ground pepper
2 tablespoons	chopped fresh parsley

1. Try to time the pasta so it is ready when the rest of the dish is done. But don't worry, this is not crucial for success. If the pasta is done early, drain it and toss with a little olive oil to keep it from sticking together.
2. Remove all traces of seeds and inner membranes, and trim any thick sections from the bell peppers. Then julienne into uniform pieces.
3. Sauté the garlic in the corn oil until golden. Add the bell peppers and sauté until they wilt.
4. Stir in the olive oil, salmon, peppercorns, salt, and pepper. Add the cooked pasta and continue to heat until the salmon warms through. Toss in the parsley and serve immediately.

Serves 4

232 CALORIES PER SERVING: 13 G PROTEIN, 11 G FAT, 19 G CARBOHYDRATE; 384 MG SODIUM; 0 MG CHOLESTEROL

Fish en Papillote

When fish is cooked wrapped in paper, it is both steamed and baked, which makes it moist and flaky (see page 92). This recipe can be prepared several hours before baking, so it is well suited to large dinner parties.

¼ cup	thinly sliced carrots
½	red bell pepper, cut into thin strips
½ to ¾ pound	fish fillet
1 tablespoon	lemon juice
1 tablespoon	minced fresh parsely
¼ teaspoon	ground coriander
	salt and pepper to taste
1 clove	garlic, crushed

1. Cut a circle of parchment paper twice the size of the fish, fold in half, then open back up.
2. Put the carrots and bell pepper on half of the paper, leaving a ½-inch margin at the outside. Set the fish on top of the vegetables and close to the inside fold mark.
3. Distribute the lemon juice, parsley, coriander, salt, and pepper on top of the fish, and set the garlic to one side of the fillet.
4. Fold the parchment paper over the fish. Seal the edges together using small, tight folds, starting on one side and working around the packet.
5. Place in an oven-proof dish and bake in a preheated 375 degree F oven. Cook thin fillets for 15 minutes and thicker ones for up to 30 minutes. Timing is not crucial because the moisture trapped in the paper packet will prevent the disaster of dried-out, overcooked fish.

Serves 2

104 CALORIES PER SERVING: 21 G PROTEIN, 1 G FAT, 3 G CARBOHYDRATE;
67 MG SODIUM; 49 MG CHOLESTEROL (analysis based on cod)

Mussels in a Shallot Sauce

A simple method with classic results. The liquid used for steaming and the juice that the mussels give off become the sauce. Serve the mussels and sauce over pasta, or simply pour the sauce over a big bowl of mussels and serve with a loaf of crusty bread.

1 large clove	garlic, crushed
½	shallot, minced (about 2 tablespoons)
2 teaspoons	olive oil
½ cup	white wine
1	large leaf fresh basil (or a dried bay leaf if fresh basil is unavailable)
	juice from 2 lemons (at least ⅔ cup)
¼ cup	water (more may be necessary, depending on the size of the pot)
2 pounds	mussels, scrubbed and debearded

1. In a pot large enough to hold all the mussels, sauté the garlic and shallot in the olive oil and some of the wine.
2. Add the rest of the wine, the basil, lemon juice, and water. When the liquid comes to a boil, reduce to a simmer and add the mussels. Cover and steam until the mussels open their shells, which will take less than 5 minutes. Discard any mussels that do not open.
3. Put the mussels into a serving bowl and cover to keep warm.
4. Strain the cooking liquid into a sauce pan, bring to a boil, and reduce by half. This takes only a couple of minutes.
5. Pour the sauce over the mussels and serve immediately.

Serves 2

144 CALORIES PER SERVING: 17 G PROTEIN, 5 G FAT, 9 G CARBOHYDRATE; 343 MG SODIUM; 60 MG CHOLESTEROL

Mussels

Mussels are inexpensive, plentiful, and delicious. A meal of mussels and pasta can be prepared, start to finish, in less than 15 minutes. Moreover, a serving of mussels has half the cholesterol of chicken and minimal amounts of saturated fat. Ocean-farmed mussels are now available in some markets. Plumper, less gritty, and guaranteed to come from clean waters, they are your best bet.

Any mussel that does not clamp shut when tapped is not alive and must be discarded. Just before steaming, thoroughly scrub the mussels and "debeard" them. The beard is the hairy strand of fibers that anchors the mussels to their moorings in the water. It is easily pulled off the shell, but should not be done too far ahead of time or the mussel will die, and eating mollusks that are not alive when cooking begins can be a serious health risk.

Figure on about 1 pound of unshucked mussels per person. They need to be steamed in ½ inch of water. Cook them quickly, and eat them immediately after cooking, when they are most tender and plump.

Cioppino

Despite the long list of ingredients, the cook's work is easy and the base, without the fish, can be made ahead of time and frozen. Chowder fish consists of inexpensive, irregularly sized cuts of fish left after fillets have been trimmed.

2 ounces	**dried Italian mushrooms (porcini are ideal)**
2 cups	**water**
2 tablespoons	**olive oil**
1	**large yellow onion, chopped**
4 cloves	**garlic, minced**
1	**green bell pepper, chopped**
28-ounce can	**whole tomatoes, drained and seeded**
¼ cup	**tomato paste**
8-ounce bottle	**clam juice**
1 cup	**white wine**
2 tablespoons	**minced fresh parsley**

2 tablespoons	chopped fresh basil, or
	2 teaspoons dried
¼ teaspoon	salt
¼ teaspoon	freshly ground pepper (or to taste)
⅛ teaspoon	red pepper flakes
2 pounds	chowder fish pieces, cut into
	1½-inch chunks
1 pound	fresh mussels or clams, or a
	combination

1. Rinse the dried mushrooms thoroughly, then soak in 1 cup warmed water, until softened (about 15 minutes). Remove the mushrooms and reserve the soaking water. Cut large mushrooms in half. Strain the soaking water through cheesecloth to remove impurities and set aside.

2. Heat the olive oil in a large pot. Add the onion, garlic, and bell pepper. Sauté until the onion becomes translucent. Add the tomatoes, tomato paste, clam juice, wine, remaining cup of water, and herbs. Stir in ¼ to ½ cup of the mushroom soaking water and the mushrooms. Simmer, covered, for 30 minutes.

3. Add the salt, pepper, red pepper flakes, and fish pieces to the pot. Cover and simmer until the fish flakes easily. (For a thinner consistency, add more of the reserved soaking water.)

4. Scrub the mollusks clean while the fish is cooking. Add them to the pot just prior to serving. They take only a couple of minutes to cook and if left in the pot too long, they turn rubbery. Discard the clams and mussels that don't open, and serve immediately.

Serves 6

290 CALORIES PER SERVING: 37 G PROTEIN, 7 G FAT, 14 G CARBOHYDRATE; 492 MG SODIUM; 120 MG CHOLESTEROL

Vegetarian Dishes

For a while it was assumed that every meal had to contain large quantities of a complete protein to be healthful and include heavy sauces to make them more appealing. It was common for foods to be served oozing with melted cheese or lavished with handfuls of nuts. Now that the problems of excess protein and fat consumption are known and accepted, getting too much has become of greater concern. A bowl of low-fat yogurt plus a few nuts and a serving of beans and rice provide more than enough protein for an average person in a day.

The following recipes offer complete meals of vegetable sauces with pastas and grains, savory casseroles, and hearty vegetable stews. All are appealing as main courses, and some can be used in smaller portions as appetizers or accompaniments to entrées.

Ethiopian Vegetables

Some years ago, while working with several Ethiopians, I gained an appreciation of their fiery hot cuisine. They start with an intense and complex base of garlic, ginger, and onion, then add other vegetables and seasonings. The flavors of the many spices meld and mellow as they simmer slowly with sweet, starchy vegetables. This is an imprecise rendition of an East African dish that I have created from memory. My Ethiopian friends would probably say it is not spicy enough. Add more cayenne if you agree.

½	small yellow onion, minced
2 cloves	garlic, minced
1 teaspoon	grated fresh ginger
2 teaspoons	vegetable oil
1	large potato, peeled and cubed, or new potatoes, unpeeled (about ¼ pound)
1	carrot, cut into rounds or cubes
1 pound	spinach, washed and coarse stems discarded
⅛ teaspoon	ground cinnamon
⅛ teaspoon	ground cardamom
⅛ to ¼ teaspoon	salt

| 1/16 teaspoon | cayenne pepper (or to taste) |
| 1/8 teaspoon | hot pepper sauce |

1. Sauté the onion, garlic, and ginger in the oil in a thick-bottomed pot. Cook slowly until the onion turns translucent.
2. Add the potato and carrot and pour in enough water to half cover the vegetables. Stir in the remaining ingredients.
3. Simmer, covered, until the potatoes and carrots start to fall apart. Stir occasionally, adding water as needed to cook the vegetables.

Serves 3

110 CALORIES PER SERVING: 6 G PROTEIN, 4 G FAT, 16 G CARBOHYDRATE;
275 MG SODIUM; 0 MG CHOLESTEROL

Dal Nepal

Prepared and cooked in less than 30 minutes, Dal Nepal has a spicy, complex flavor and an attractive pale orange color.

3 cloves	garlic, minced
1/2 tablespoon	grated fresh ginger
1	medium yellow onion, minced
1 tablespoon	vegetable oil
1 cup	red lentils
3 cups	water
1 teaspoon	ground turmeric
2 teaspoons	ground cumin
2 teaspoons	chili powder
1/4 teaspoon	hot pepper sauce (or to taste)

1. Sauté the garlic, ginger, and onion in the oil over low heat until thoroughly cooked.
2. Add the remaining ingredients and simmer, uncovered, for 20 minutes.
3. Taste and adjust the seasonings, and serve.

Serves 6

55 CALORIES PER 1/2 CUP: 2 G PROTEIN, 3 G FAT, 5 G CARBOHYDRATE;
13 MG SODIUM; 0 MG CHOLESTEROL

Chick-Pea Curry

Even people who insist that they hate curry love this recipe. It is on the mild side and uses the sweeter curry spices. Small bowls of condiments are often served with curries so guests can garnish their plates to their own liking.

3 cloves	garlic, minced
2 teaspoons	minced fresh ginger
1 to 2	leeks, white part only, minced (use onions or scallions if leeks are unavailable)
2 teaspoons	vegetable oil
1½ cups	peeled, grated butternut squash (grates easily in food processor)
1	carrot, shredded
2	medium all-purpose potatoes, peeled and cubed
2 cups	water
4 cups	cooked chick-peas
1½ to 2 teaspoons	curry powder
½ teaspoon	ground coriander
⅛ teaspoon	cayenne pepper
¼ teaspoon	salt
1	apple, peeled and chopped raisins, apples, and toasted nuts for condiments

1. Sauté the garlic, ginger, and leeks in the oil over low heat until soft.
2. Add the squash, carrot, and potatoes. Pour in the water and simmer, covered, until the vegetables soften. If neccessary, add more water so that the curry doesn't stick to the bottom of the pot.
3. Add all but the apple and cook for 30 minutes longer.
4. Ten minutes before serving, add the apple. Taste and adjust the seasonings, if necessary.

Serves 6

186 CALORIES PER CUP: 6 G PROTEIN, 4 G FAT, 34 G CARBOHYDRATE; 504 MG SODIUM; 0 MG CHOLESTEROL

Mediterranean Baked Beans

I use a cast-iron pot for this because it can go from the stove top directly into the oven; it also heats very evenly and keeps the beans from drying out. If you prefer, you can do all the cooking on the stove top, but beans are at their very best when baked for a long time.

2 cups	navy or other white beans, washed, then soaked overnight in 6 cups water
4 cups	water or stock
2	bay leaves
3 cloves	garlic, peeled and crushed
3 tablespoons	minced fresh parsley
2 teaspoons	dried dill
½ teaspoon	salt
1½ cups	crushed tomatoes
1 cup	tomato juice
1 cup	chopped celery (about 2 ribs)
5	peperoncini, rinsed and chopped (these are pickled spicy Italian peppers found in the international food section of your market)
¼ teaspoon	freshly ground pepper

1. Drain the soaking liquid from the beans.
2. Put 4 cups fresh water into a pot with the beans, bay leaves, and garlic.
3. Simmer for about 45 minutes, or until the skins on the beans begin to break.
4. Stir in the remaining ingredients and pour into an oven-proof casserole. Bake, covered, in a preheated 350 degree F oven for 2 hours. Stir the beans several times as they bake. If they start to dry out, lower the heat and add more water.

Serves 6

134 CALORIES PER SERVING: 8 G PROTEIN, 1 G FAT, 25 G CARBOHYDRATE; 189 MG SODIUM; 0 MG CHOLESTEROL

Caponata

This spicy Sicilian eggplant dish is wonderful served hot as the main event, or at room temperature, finely chopped, as an appetizer with whole wheat crackers for scooping.

3 cloves	garlic, minced
1 cup	chopped onion
⅓ cup	red wine
1 rib	celery, chopped
1	medium eggplant, cut into small cubes
28-ounce can	whole tomatoes
2 tablespoons	red wine vinegar
1 tablespoon	malt syrup
1 tablespoon	dried basil
1 teaspoon	capers
6 drops	hot pepper sauce
¼ to ½ teaspoon	salt (depends on how salty the canned tomatoes are)

1. Sauté the garlic and onion in the red wine over low heat until softened. Cover between stirrings.
2. Add the celery and eggplant and cook slowly until the eggplant softens. This will take at least 15 minutes. If more liquid is needed, add juice from the canned tomatoes.
3. Add remaining ingredients and simmer at least 30 minutes, longer if time permits.

Serves 4

73 CALORIES PER SERVING: 2 G PROTEIN, 1 G FAT, 15 G CARBOHYDRATE; 321 MG SODIUM; 0 MG CHOLESTEROL

Capers

Capers look a lot like green peppercorns, but they have a flavor unlike anything else. They are the pickled flowering buds of a shrub that grows in the Mediterranean. Capers come in two sizes, with the smaller ones being preferable. Most supermarkets stock capers, either in the international foods section or with the spices.

Bean Enchiladas

Enchiladas freeze well and can be reheated in the microwave or in a nonstick pan on the stove top. The ingredients can also be frozen separately. With tortillas, plain-cooked beans, and enchilada sauce in the freezer, this dish can be made in no time.

¼	Spanish onion, chopped (½ cup)
2 cloves	garlic, minced
½	green bell pepper, minced (½ cup)
1 tablespoon	vegetable oil
1 teaspoon	ground coriander
½ teaspoon	chili powder
6 drops	hot pepper sauce
6 cups	cooked pinto beans
3½ cups	Enchilada Sauce (recipe follows)
10 to 12	corn tortillas

1. Sauté the onion, garlic, and bell pepper in the oil. As they cook, stir in the spices.
2. Mix the sautéed ingredients with half the beans.
3. Mash or puree the remaining beans, then add to the whole-bean mixture.
4. Spread 3 cups of the enchilada sauce on the bottom of an oblong baking pan.
5. Place ⅓ cup bean mixture on a tortilla and roll it up. (To keep the corn tortillas from cracking, stack them in a dish with a little water in the bottom. Use the tortillas, starting with the one sitting in the water. This keeps them pliable, but not soggy.)
6. Set each rolled tortilla into the baking pan, seam side down. Leave a little space between each one for easy removal after baking.
7. After all the tortillas are rolled and in the pan, drizzle the remaining enchilada sauce over them, but do not cover the tortillas completely.
8. Cover and bake in a 375 degree F oven for 45 minutes. If foil is used to cover the pan, take care that it doesn't touch the sauce because the acid in tomatoes will react with the foil.

Makes 10 to 12 enchiladas

278 CALORIES PER ENCHILADA: 13 G PROTEIN, 3 G FAT, 52 G CARBOHYDRATE; 223 MG SODIUM; 0 MG CHOLESTEROL

Enchilada Sauce

This is flavorful but not too hot. Cumin is one of those spices that you either love or hate, so add more or omit it, according to your preference. For accompaniments, serve Hot! Sauce and Almost Sour Cream (pages 186 and 185, respectively).

1	medium yellow onion, minced (½ cup)
½	green bell pepper, minced (½ cup)
2 cloves	garlic, minced
½ cup	red wine
¼ teaspoon	salt
1 tablespoon	chili powder
¼ to ½ teaspoon	ground cumin
6 cups	tomato puree
2 cups	ground peeled tomatoes

1. Sauté the onion, bell pepper, and garlic in the wine until the vegetables are soft.
2. Add the rest of the ingredients, cover, and simmer for at least 30 minutes.

Yields 7 cups (enough for 2 batches of enchiladas)

54 CALORIES PER ½ CUP: 2 G PROTEIN, 0 G FAT, 13 G CARBOHYDRATE; 479 MG SODIUM; 0 MG CHOLESTEROL

Chili

My version of this hotly debated bean dish is vegetarian, which is heresy to some and gospel to others. If it simply does not seem right without meat, add a little browned ground turkey.

2 cloves	garlic, minced
1	medium onion, chopped
2 tablespoons	soy sauce
2 teaspoons	vegetable oil
½ cup	water
1	green bell pepper, chopped
1 to 2	mild green chili peppers, rinsed and cleaned (these come canned and sometimes already chopped)

1 teaspoon	dried oregano
½ teaspoon	ground coriander
1½ tablespoons	chili powder (or more to taste)
	cayenne pepper to taste (start with ⅛ teaspoon)
28-ounce can	whole peeled tomatoes
4 cups	cooked red kidney beans

1. Sauté the garlic and onion in the soy sauce and oil. Add a little water if it begins to scorch. Stir in the green bell pepper and the rest of the water and cook until soft. Stir in the chili peppers, herbs, and spices.
2. Drain and chop the tomatoes (reserving liquid) and add them to the pot. Add the beans.
3. Simmer at least 45 minutes, the longer the better. If cooking for several hours, use the reserved juice from the canned tomatoes if additional liquid is needed.

Serves 6

214 CALORIES PER SERVING: 12 G PROTEIN, 3 G FAT, 38 G CARBOHYDRATE; 676 MG SODIUM; 0 MG CHOLESTEROL

Stuffed Vegetables

Any vegetable that naturally hollows out is a good candidate for stuffing, although the most common are winter squashes, such as acorn and butternut. Because these are hard vegetables, they require partial cooking before stuffing. The microwave can do this in less than 15 minutes, but I believe squash tastes best when baked. To bake squash, cut it in half, scoop out the seeds, and remove some of the flesh if a larger cavity is desired. Place the squash cut side down on a baking tray and bake in a preheated 375 degree F oven until tender. Don't overcook since it will be heated a second time with the filling.

Softer vegetables, such as bell peppers and summer squash, also make good containers for stuffings. These, too, need to be softened prior to stuffing but this can be done quickly by steaming.

Squash with Wild Rice Stuffing

This rice mixture is so nice that you can serve it as a side dish, or even chilled as a salad.

½ cup	wild rice
1¼ cups	stock or water
2 cloves	garlic, chopped
½ tablespoon	minced shallots
1	small leek, minced
	olive oil for sautéing
1 rib	celery, minced, including leaves
½ teaspoon	orange zest
1	orange, peeled, membranes removed, and segmented
¼ cup	pecans, toasted and chopped
	salt and pepper to taste
½ tablespoon	sherry
1	egg white, lightly beaten
2	summer or winter squashes, halved, seeded, and steamed or baked to soften

1. Cook the wild rice in the stock until all of the liquid is absorbed (about 50 minutes). (Some varieties of rice come partially cooked and need less liquid, so if your rice came in a box, read the directions carefully and add as much liquid as is suggested.)
2. Sauté the garlic, shallots, and leek in enough olive oil to lightly coat the bottom of a pan. Add the celery and sauté for a few more minutes.
3. Combine the cooked rice, sautéed vegetables, orange zest, orange, pecans, salt, pepper, sherry, and egg white.
4. Spoon stuffing into squashes and place in a baking pan so that they are not touching. Add about ¼ inch of water to bottom of pan. Bake in a preheated 375 degree F oven for 30 minutes.

Serves 4

290 CALORIES PER SERVING: 10 G PROTEIN, 6 G FAT, 52 G CARBOHYDRATE; 35 MG SODIUM; 0 MG CHOLESTEROL (analysis based on acorn squash)

Millet or Quinoa Stuffed Squash

Yes, this harkens back to the granola days of the early '70s, but it is good all the same. Some people think of meat, potatoes, and gravy as comfort food, but I think of stuffed squash. Here, the sweetness of acorn squash is complemented by the mildness of cottage cheese and the zip of chives. The texture is soft, not mushy. Because squashes don't come in consistent sizes, you may have more than enough stuffing. Either hollow out the squash to accommodate more, or put the excess into a casserole dish or whatever else is handy, such as a bell pepper, and bake it along with the squash.

1	large squash or 2 medium
1 cup	cooked millet or quinoa
1	egg white, beaten
1 cup	low-fat cottage cheese
¼ cup	minced fresh chives
1 clove	garlic, minced
½ teaspoon	dried marjoram
¼ teaspoon	freshly ground pepper
1 tablespoon	grated Parmesan cheese
	paprika, fresh chives, or parsley
	for garnish

1. Cut the squash in half. Scoop out the seeds. Slice off a sliver of the squash from its bottom so it will sit flat. Steam, bake, or microwave until tender. (Baking will bring out the best flavor in winter squash.)
2. Combine the remaining ingredients and spoon enough into the squash for a nicely shaped mound on top.
3. Place in a baking pan with ¼ inch of water on the bottom (this will keep squash from drying out). Cover loosely and bake in a preheated 350 degree F oven for 30 minutes. Uncover and bake for 5–10 minutes longer. Garnish as desired. If using large squash, cut in half again before serving.

Serves 4

141 CALORIES PER SERVING: 12 G PROTEIN, 2 G FAT, 19 G CARBOHYDRATE; 276 MG SODIUM; 4 MG CHOLESTEROL

Mushroom Lasagna

I use a combination of low-fat, partially low-fat, and full-fat cheeses in my lasagna, and the fat content is still under 20%. In fact, those who like their lasagna with melted cheese can put a thin layer of part-skim milk mozzarella on top, and this recipe will still be less than 30% fat. One of the cheeses used here is farmer's cheese. It looks like dry cottage cheese but is sweeter and softer. Because it is low in moisture, it is excellent for baking. If unavailable, use cottage cheese with the excess water drained off, or pureed tofu for a denser filling.

1 pound	farmer's cheese
½ pound	low-fat ricotta
2	egg whites
⅛ cup	grated Parmesan cheese
1 tablespoon	fresh chives
1 tablespoon	minced fresh parsley
¼ teaspoon	freshly ground pepper
10-ounce package	lasagna noodles
1	yellow onion, minced (1 cup)
¼ cup	red wine
1½ pounds	mushrooms, sliced
4 cups	Red Sauce (page 115)

1. Puree the farmer's cheese, ricotta, egg whites, and Parmesan. Blend in the chives, parsley, and pepper by hand.
2. Boil the lasagna noodles until just cooked, not mushy (about 5 minutes). Lay out flat on clean kitchen towels (not paper!) to keep the noodles from sticking together.
3. Simmer the onion in the wine until very soft. Stir frequently, but keep the pot covered in between stirrings.
4. Add the mushrooms to the onions and cook until they wilt and are half the original volume. This will take about 5 minutes. Drain the vegetables and discard the liquid.
5. Combine the pureed cheese mixture and all but ¼ cup of the mushrooms.
6. Spread 2 cups of the red sauce in the bottom of a 9-inch by 12-inch baking pan. Then layer in this order: noodles, cheese, noodles, cheese, noodles, remaining red sauce.
7. Distribute the reserved mushrooms over the top.
8. Bake, covered, in a preheated 375 degree F oven for 1 hour. Uncover and cook for 5 minutes longer.

9. Remove from the oven and let rest for 10 minutes before cutting.

Serves 9

235 CALORIES PER SERVING: 22 G PROTEIN, 4 G FAT, 29 G CARBOHYDRATE;
523 MG SODIUM; 13 MG CHOLESTEROL

Red Sauce

A most versatile sauce to have on hand. Ladle it on top of pasta, with a scant grating of Parmesan cheese, for a main dish. Reheat chicken in it, add a sliced green bell pepper, and you have another dinner. Toss it with vegetables and some fresh basil for a side dish. This oil-free recipe can easily be doubled, and it freezes very well.

3 large cloves	garlic, minced
¼	Spanish onion, or 1 small yellow onion, minced
1 rib	celery, minced
⅓ cup	red wine
3½ cups	tomato puree (28-ounce can)
1½ cups	canned whole peeled tomatoes, coarsely chopped, with the juice
1 tablespoon	dried basil
2 teaspoons	dried oregano
¼ teaspoon	dried rosemary
1 tablespoon	minced fresh parsley
1	bay leaf
1	peeled whole carrot
⅛ teaspoon	salt

1. Briefly sauté the garlic, onion, and celery in a little of the wine, then add the rest of the wine, cover, and simmer for 10 minutes. If more liquid is needed, use the juice from the canned tomatoes.
2. Add the remaining ingredients and continue to simmer at least 30 minutes longer. The longer this cooks, the better it will taste. If there's time, let it sit overnight in the refrigerator.
3. Before serving, discard the bay leaf and the carrot.

Yields 5 cups

50 CALORIES PER ½ CUP: 2 G PROTEIN, 0 G FAT, 11 G CARBOHYDRATE;
411 MG SODIUM; 0 MG CHOLESTEROL

Tomato Coulis

The simplest imaginable sauce is a coulis—a quickly prepared vegetable puree—and the most basic of these is the tomato coulis. There are no hard-and-fast rules for making a coulis, except that the ingredients must be the freshest and the best. A coulis is versatile. It can be served hot or cold, on pasta or meat, or with other vegetables.

1 tablespoon	olive oil
1 pound	ripe tomatoes, chopped
2 tablespoons	chopped shallots (about 1 large)
1 clove	garlic, minced
⅛ teaspoon	salt
¼ teaspoon	freshly ground pepper

1. Heat the oil in a pan.
2. Stir in all the ingredients, then cover.
3. Cook for 5–7 minutes, stirring occasionally.
4. Cool the sauce, then pour into a food processor fitted with metal blade and chop until it is in small lumps. Serve as desired.

Yields 1⅓ cups

57 CALORIES PER ⅓ CUP: 1 G PROTEIN, 4 G FAT, 6 G CARBOHYDRATE; 77 MG SODIUM; 0 MG CHOLESTEROL

Mushroom and Tomato Sauce

Here's another tomato-based sauce, which is especially good served over pasta or brown rice. The mushrooms contribute a meaty texture, and the capers, a hint of the Mediterranean.

1 tablespoon	olive oil
1 large clove	garlic, minced
½	large Spanish onion, minced
12 ounces	thickly sliced mushrooms (4 cups)
⅓ cup	red wine
¼ cup	minced fresh parsley
28-ounce can	whole tomatoes, coarsely chopped
2	bay leaves
1 tablespoon	dried basil, or 3 tablespoons fresh
2 teaspoons	capers, rinsed
½ tablespoon	soy sauce
	freshly ground pepper to taste

1. Heat the oil in a heavy, non-metallic pot.
2. Sauté the garlic and onion in the oil until the onion turns lightly golden. Add the mushrooms and wine, cover, and cook until the mushrooms shrink in size and are soft. Stir occasionally.
3. Add the remaining ingredients and cook for at least 1 hour—longer if possible.

Serves 4

120 CALORIES PER SERVING: 4 G PROTEIN, 4 G FAT, 16 G CARBOHYDRATE; 469 MG SODIUM; 0 MG CHOLESTEROL

Basil Pesto

Pesto is an intensely flavored, versatile sauce that can add life to a whole bowl of pasta or a steamed bunch of broccoli. It is the ultimate fast food, and can be made in a few minutes in a blender or food processor. It will last a week in the refrigerator, for months in the freezer.

2 cups	fresh basil leaves (not dried)
2 cloves	garlic
½ cup	pine nuts, or walnuts
2 tablespoons	grated Romano cheese
5 tablespoons	grated Parmesan cheese
5 tablespoons	olive oil

1. Wash the basil leaves carefully and dry thoroughly.
2. In a blender or food processor fitted with metal blade, puree the ingredients in the order listed, scraping down the sides of the processor after each is chopped. (The mixture will not be smooth until the oil is added.) With the machine running, slowly add the oil in a thin, steady stream. As soon as it is smoothly incorporated, the pesto is ready.

A serving suggestion: Cook up enough pasta for 2 people. Combine 1 teaspoon olive oil with 1 tablespoon pesto and toss with the hot pasta. Top with toasted pine nuts and chopped ripe tomatoes. Garnish with freshly ground pepper.

Makes approximately 1½ cups

102 CALORIES PER 2 TABLESPOONS: 2.5 G PROTEIN, 10 G FAT, 2 G CARBOHYDRATE; 61 MG SODIUM; 3 MG CHOLESTEROL

Spinach and Friends

Spinach gets together with tomatoes, garlic, and nubby pasta for a good time. The cook should have a good time, too, for the only step that takes a while is washing the spinach.

½ pound	fresh spinach
1½ tablespoons	olive oil
1 clove	garlic, minced (about 1 teaspoon)
½ pound	fresh tomatoes, peeled and thickly sliced (these must be truly ripe and flavorful)
¼ teaspoon	salt
¼ teaspoon	freshly ground pepper (or to taste)
4 ounces	dried pasta (short and nubby is best) freshly grated Parmesan cheese for garnish (optional)

1. Wash the spinach well, removing tough stems, but do not dry thoroughly. The water clinging to the leaves provides the liquid for cooking. If you can find it, buy flat, broad-leafed spinach, but the crinkly, cellophane-wrapped spinach will do.
2. Heat the oil in a pot large enough to hold all the spinach. Add the garlic and sauté until golden.
3. Put in the spinach, cover, and cook briefly until wilted. Stir once or twice during cooking.
4. Add the tomatoes and cook until softened. Stir in the salt and pepper and keep the sauce warm on low heat.
5. Cook the pasta. As soon as it is done, drain it and toss with the sauce.
6. Grate Parmesan cheese on top of each serving, if desired.

Serves 2

304 CALORIES PER SERVING: 10 G PROTEIN, 12 G FAT, 44 G CARBOHYDRATE; 366 MG SODIUM; 0 MG CHOLESTEROL

Broccoli and Garlic Pasta

I cook this up when I'm hungry and haven't planned anything for dinner. I usually have broccoli (or another green vegetable) on hand, and there's always garlic and pasta in the pantry. If I have pesto or red sauce around, I stir that in as the broccoli cooks. To keep the amount of oil to a minimum and to speed cooking, I use my wok or a nonstick pan that cooks evenly and quickly. (Try not to eat this out of the pot, even if you're ravenously hungry. It is too easy for a single diner to lose the visual pleasure of an attractively presented meal.)

1 teaspoon	olive oil
1 large clove	garlic, minced
1 tablespoon	onion, chopped
1 tablespoon	white wine
4 tablespoons	or more chicken or vegetable stock (if stock has been frozen in ice cube trays, use 2 cubes to equal 4 tablespoons)
	broccoli spears for 1 person
	cooked pasta for 1 person
	salt and pepper to taste
2 teaspoons	freshly grated Parmesan or Romano cheese

1. Heat the oil in a wok or nonstick pan. Add the garlic and onion and sauté over low heat until the onion becomes translucent.
2. Add the wine, stock, and broccoli. (You can use leftover, lightly steamed broccoli.) Cover and cook until the broccoli turns bright green.
3. Toss in the pasta and cook until it is heated through and the broccoli is tender.
4. Season with salt and pepper. Turn out onto a dish and dust the top with the cheese.

Serves 1

275 CALORIES PER SERVING: 11 G PROTEIN, 7 G FAT, 44 G CARBOHYDRATE; 107 MG SODIUM; 3 MG CHOLESTEROL

Spicy Tofu

The texture of tofu is vastly improved by marinating and baking. I originally used the cubes as a sandwich stuffing, but my students came up with many more uses. They toss them into salads and pasta dishes, serve them as snacks, and put them into stir-fries. Another inventive marinade for tofu is the Indonesian Sauce (see page 84).

1 pound	firm tofu, drained
1½ tablespoons	soy sauce
¼ teaspoon	dry mustard
1 teaspoon	dried oregano

1. Cut the block of tofu into small cubes.
2. Toss the tofu in a bowl with soy sauce, mustard, and oregano. Marinate for at least 15 minutes or as long as 1 day.
3. Line a baking sheet with parchment paper. Put the tofu cubes on the sheet. They can be close, but not touching.
4. Bake in a preheated 450 degree F oven for 10 minutes, then shake the pan to loosen the cubes from the paper. Continue to bake, about 10–15 minutes longer, until the outside of the tofu browns and crisps but the inside remains soft. Use as desired.

Serves 8

86 CALORIES PER SERVING: 9 G PROTEIN, 5 G FAT, 3 G CARBOHYDRATE; 201 MG SODIUM; 0 MG CHOLESTEROL

Chinese Dumpling Rolls

These dumplings are similar to eggrolls, but they are steamed, not fried. And although they can be shaped like dumplings, they aren't exactly dumplings either. Instead, they are a combination of the two. I eat them for lunch, for dinner, or serve little ones as hors d'oeuvres. I change the fillings to suit my mood or to use what is on hand.

1 teaspoon	grated fresh ginger
2	scallions, thinly sliced
½ cup	firm tofu, crumbled
1 cup	shredded bok choy or other Chinese cabbage

½ cup	bean sprouts
½ cup	sliced mushrooms (shiitakes will add an oriental flavor)
	oil for sautéing
½ cup	cooked brown rice
1	egg white, lightly beaten
1 tablespoon	soy sauce
½ teaspoon	mirin (a sweet cooking wine; sherry can be substituted)
¾ teaspoon	toasted sesame oil
1 package	eggroll, spring roll, or wonton wrappers
	hot mustard as accompaniment

1. Combine the first 6 ingredients. Sauté in a wok or skillet with a touch of oil, and cook until the cabbage softens.
2. Mix well with the rice, egg white, soy sauce, mirin, and sesame oil.
3. Spoon a portion of this filling into the lower half of a wrapper and fold eggroll fashion (eggroll wrappers can be cut in half to make appetizer-sized portions if desired). Or wet the edges of a wrapper and fold over so the edges meet. Press the edges together and seal with the tines of a fork.
4. Line a steamer basket with parchment paper or lettuce or cabbage leaves (this keeps the dumplings from sticking). Set the filled dumplings in the basket over boiling water and steam for 10 minutes.
5. The dumplings can be served at this point, or crisped to a light brown by cooking them in a little oil (about a teaspoon) for 1 minute on each side.
6. Serve with hot mustard.

Makes 12 large dumplings

45 CALORIES PER DUMPLING: 3 G PROTEIN, 1 G FAT, 6 G CARBOHYDRATE; 113 MG SODIUM; 0 MG CHOLESTEROL

TO ROUND
IT OUT
Vegetables, Grains, and Pastas

I decided not to label this chapter "Side Dishes" because I didn't want to give these recipes short shrift. Many people think of side dishes as secondary foods, when in essence, they are no less important than the entrée.

Chicken or fish may be the focal point of a meal, but it is the serving of vegetable, grain, or pasta that should fill you up. I'm always disappointed with restaurants that serve a large piece of meat but only two small potatoes and a bite-sized vegetable. It is like looking through a telescope from the wrong end: the picture is right but the perspective is wrong.

A Single Person's Approach to Fresh Vegetables

When a single individual buys a bunch of broccoli, it is often difficult to consume the entire vegetable before it grows limp and becomes inedible. This is one reason why many single people resign themselves to eating only frozen vegetables, or worse—no vegetables at all. There are ways around this problem, however. One solution is to lightly steam the whole head of broccoli. Steamed vegetables get eaten faster than raw. They not only can be heated up quickly, but also can be used as ingredients for other meals.

Try this: the first day, serve fresh broccoli steamed as a vegetable side dish. The next day, toss some of the steamed broccoli into a green luncheon salad. That evening, munch on florets as a snack with dip, and later use some of the broccoli in a stir-fry. For lunch the next day, assemble a vegetable salad with broccoli that has been marinated in a favorite salad dressing (which is just what those fancy gourmet take-out food stores do when making expensive marinated vegetable salads). Whip up a fast pasta dinner by sautéing onion, garlic, and broccoli in olive oil, and then tossing this with pasta and cracked pepper. If, after all this, there is still some broccoli left over, add it to a soup.

Thus, with a little forethought and creativity the single person can avoid those wilted vegetables blues.

Broccoli and Roasted Peppers

Pungent garlic and smoky roasted peppers meet the king of the cabbage family in this gutsy dish. Toss in some pasta and a tablespoon of grated Parmesan cheese and you have dinner.

1 clove	garlic, minced
1 teaspoon	olive oil
1 cup	julienned Roasted Peppers (recipe follows)
2	large servings broccoli spears, lightly steamed
2 tablespoons	or more vegetable or chicken stock
	salt and pepper to taste

1. Sauté the garlic in the oil over low heat until the garlic turns light golden.
2. Stir in the roasted pepper and cook briefly. Add the broccoli. At this point more liquid will be needed both to heat the broccoli and keep it moist. Start with 2 tablespoons, but add more if necessary. Cover the vegetables and cook, stirring every few minutes, until the broccoli is hot and the desired texture. (If you have stock frozen into ice cubes, this is a good time to use some. Put a couple right into the pan. The stock will melt quickly, and the steam will warm and soften the broccoli.)
3. Season with salt and pepper, and serve.

Serves 2

77 CALORIES PER SERVING: 5 G PROTEIN, 3 G FAT, 11 G CARBOHYDRATE; 18 MG SODIUM; 0 MG CHOLESTEROL

Roasted Peppers

Roasting transforms peppers: they become velvety smooth, rustic and rich, sweet, yet earthy. Roasted peppers can be made from any color pepper. A mixture of red, yellow, and green is both festive and flavorful. Stored in a jar, roasted peppers will keep for several days; covered in olive oil, for a couple of weeks. Use them in pasta or leafy salads, alongside grilled fish or chicken, in an antipasto, or as a filling for a pita pocket sandwich.

4   bell peppers (more or less), any color

1. Preheat the broiler. Line the broiler pan or rack with foil because the peppers will drip.
2. Place the peppers under the heating element, close but not touching. Broil until the skins char. Let them get black, otherwise the skins won't peel off. Turn the peppers (using long-handled tongs!) until all sides are blackened.
3. Put the peppers in a paper bag, close it up, and let the peppers cool. The steam from the peppers will moisten the bag, but will also make the skins removable. The bottom may tear open, so be careful if you move the bag.
4. Hold the peppers under cool running water while you slip off the skins.
5. Cut open the peppers and remove the seeds, stem, and whitish ribs. For most uses the peppers should be cut into strips.

Yields about 3 cups

12 CALORIES PER ½ CUP SERVING: 0 G PROTEIN, 0 G FAT, 3 G CARBOHYDRATE;
1 MG SODIUM; 0 MG CHOLESTEROL

Great Green Beans

Green beans are one of my very favorite vegetables. I eat them steamed, chilled as a snack, or in a marinated salad. This is the recipe I use when I want to dress them up; in fact, Great Green Beans can become a quick dinner piled over a bed of couscous or brown rice, and topped with a grating of good, aged Parmesan cheese. It is essential that you use fresh beans—those that are smooth, unblemished, and with lots of "snap."

2 teaspoons	vegetable or olive oil
1	small yellow onion, chopped (½ cup)
1 teaspoon	balsamic vinegar
3	plum or 2 beefsteak tomatoes, peeled, seeded, and chopped (see page 63)
2 tablespoons	white wine
⅛ teaspoon	salt
¼ teaspoon	freshly ground pepper
2 tablespoons	minced fresh parsley
¼ teaspoon	dried oregano
½ pound	fresh green beans, washed and ends trimmed

1. In a medium-sized sauté pan, heat the oil, add the onion, and sauté until softened. Add the vinegar and cook over low heat, stirring frequently, until the onion begins to turn a light golden color and starts to caramelize (this long cooking brings out the sweetness of the onion and thickens the vinegar).
2. Add the tomatoes, wine, and seasonings. Cook, covered, until the tomatoes are warmed through. If more liquid is needed, add a tablespoon or so of wine.
3. Meanwhile, steam the beans until crisp-tender, then toss with the sauce and serve.

Serves 4

57 CALORIES PER SERVING: 2 G PROTEIN, 3 G FAT, 8 G CARBOHYDRATE; 73 MG SODIUM; 0 MG CHOLESTEROL

Baked Tomatoes

I've always liked broiled tomatoes but baked are even better. The longer baking time softens and sweetens them, creating a traditional, old-fashioned, gratifying dish. This recipe contains no butter, just a touch of olive oil; it can be prepared well ahead of time and can easily be doubled.

4	ripe tomatoes
¼ cup	bread crumbs (see page 87)
2 tablespoons	minced fresh parsley
1 tablespoon	sherry or sweet white wine
1 teaspoon	olive oil
⅛ teaspoon	freshly ground pepper
	salt

1. Using a paring knife, cut a line of connected V's about a fifth of the way down from the core of each tomato. Then pull the tops off, leaving beautifully serrated edges. If necessary, slice a tiny bit off the bottoms of the tomatoes so they will not roll around.
2. Combine the bread crumbs, parsley, wine, and oil.
3. Grate pepper on the cut tomato and shake a light amount of salt on, too.
4. Divide the breading into 4 portions and mound on top of each tomato. Lightly pack it down. Place the tomatoes on a baking sheet or in a shallow casserole dish.
5. Bake the tomatoes in a preheated oven until they are cooked throughout, about 20 minutes. (Use whatever temperature is required for the rest of the meal: anywhere from 325 to 375 degrees F.)

Serves 4

69 CALORIES PER SERVING: 2 G PROTEIN, 2 G FAT, 11 G CARBOHYDRATE; 124 MG SODIUM; 0 MG CHOLESTEROL

TO ROUND IT OUT

Cheery Cherry Tomatoes

Terrific served hot right out of the pan, or chilled and added to leafy green salads.

1 tablespoon	corn oil
1 clove	garlic, minced
1 tablespoon	minced shallots (about ½ large bulb)
1 pint	cherry tomatoes
⅛ teaspoon	salt (optional)
¼ teaspoon	freshly ground pepper

1. Heat a sauté pan, pour in the oil, and roll it around the pan so the surface is well coated.
2. Cook the garlic and shallots on low heat until golden.
3. Turn the heat to high and add the tomatoes, salt, and pepper. Toss continually until the skins pop open. This takes only about 1 minute.

Serves 6

34 CALORIES PER SERVING: 1 G PROTEIN, 2 G FAT, 3 G CARBOHYDRATE; 5 MG SODIUM; 0 MG CHOLESTEROL

Asparagus with Warm Lemon Dressing

Fresh asparagus requires little more than simply steaming it to the desired tenderness; however, this light dressing just adds to the pleasure. Any leftovers can be used as a chilled asparagus salad.

1 pound	asparagus
1	shallot, peeled and crushed
1 clove	garlic, peeled and crushed
2 teaspoons	olive oil
2 tablespoons	white wine
1 tablespoon	lemon juice
⅛ to ¼ teaspoon	freshly ground pepper

1. Wash the asparagus, then snap off and discard the tough bottoms by bending the stalk until it breaks. This should happen where the fibrous part ends and the tender green shoot begins. If the stalks are thick, peel the bottom third.

2. Steam the asparagus until tender.
3. Meanwhile, sauté the shallot and garlic in the olive oil and wine over low heat until the alcohol evaporates and the garlic turns golden. This takes about 10 minutes. Discard the garlic and shallot.
4. Whisk the lemon juice and pepper into the oil and wine, pour over the steamed asparagus, and serve.

Serves 4

49 CALORIES PER SERVING: 3 G PROTEIN, 3 G FAT, 5 G CARBOHYDRATE; 3 MG SODIUM; 0 MG CHOLESTEROL

Sautéed Summer Vegetables

This can accompany a main dish or be served as the main course over couscous, rice, or pasta. For protein, add a light grating of cheese. Choose small, firm squashes for best results.

½	yellow onion, sliced
1 teaspoon	olive oil
½	green pepper, sliced
1	yellow squash, thickly sliced
1	zucchini, thickly sliced
1	tomato, chopped
½ teaspoon	dried oregano
1 teaspoon	dried basil
	freshly ground pepper

1. Sauté the onion in the olive oil over low heat until soft and translucent.
2. Add the green pepper and cook until it wilts.
3. Add the yellow squash, zucchini, and tomato, and cook, covered, for 10 minutes.
4. Stir in the herbs and the pepper, and serve.

Serves 4

40 CALORIES PER SERVING: 1 G PROTEIN, 2 G FAT, 6 G CARBOHYDRATE; 4 MG SODIUM; 0 MG CHOLESTEROL

Baked Beets

If you are lucky enough to find beets with fresh, unblemished greens still attached, buy them! All the greens need is a good washing and a quick steaming, or prepare them as described in Steamed Beet Greens with Sesame Oil (recipe follows). The beets, themselves, are also easy to cook, but require more time: about an hour in a conventional oven or 15 minutes in a microwave.

1 pound	fresh beets
1 tablespoon	water
¼ teaspoon	ground nutmeg

1. Cut off the tops and tails of the beets. Large beets need to have their tough skins peeled, but small ones just need a good scrubbing. (I use rubber gloves when working with beets so that my hands don't get dyed purple.)
2. Place beets in a casserole dish, sprinkle with the water and nutmeg, and cover.
3. Bake in a preheated 350 degree F oven for 1 hour, or until tender.

Serves 4

35 CALORIES PER SERVING: 1 G PROTEIN, 0 G FAT, 8 G CARBOHYDRATE; 56 MG SODIUM; 0 MG CHOLESTEROL

Steamed Beet Greens with Sesame Oil

Beet greens are a dark, leafy vegetable with ruby veins. Their delicate flavor in this recipe is enhanced by the toasted sesame oil, an essential ingredient. Don't substitute plain sesame oil—it won't do.

½ pound	fresh beet greens
¼ teaspoon	toasted sesame oil (not plain sesame oil)
⅛ to ¼ teaspoon	soy sauce
½ teaspoon	toasted sesame seeds

1. Wash the greens thoroughly to cleanse them of dirt and grit. Snap off the bottom, tough ends of the stems, and gently remove those parts of the leaves that are brownish or wilted.

2. Place greens in a steamer basket set over rapidly boiling water. Cover and cook for about 2 minutes, or until they are wilted and a rich green color.
3. Toss greens in a bowl with the toasted sesame oil and soy sauce. Top with sesame seeds and serve.

Serves 3

22 CALORIES PER SERVING: 2 G PROTEIN, 1 G FAT, 3 G CARBOHYDRATE; 180 MG SODIUM; 0 MG CHOLESTEROL

Carrots and Peas

My father's idea of the height of culinary expertise is the New Jersey diner. Because of this, I ate lots of cubed carrots and peas when I was growing up. Years later, when I was training to be a chef, I was taught how to cut carrots into those perfect tiny cubes. I rank that skill with the most important I've learned, and share the technique here. You *can* make this dish with carrots sliced into rounds—but those little cubes fit on a fork so nicely. Remember?

1 cup	cubed carrots
½ cup	fresh peas
	freshly ground pepper (optional)
	minced fresh mint or dill (optional)

1. Place the carrots in a steamer over rapidly boiling water and steam for 5 minutes.
2. Add the peas to the steamer and heat through. Toss peas and carrots in a bowl with pepper and herb, if desired.

Note: To cube a carrot, slice it along its length several times. Then cut those pieces lengthwise again, creating strips that are approximately the same width. Put these back into the carrot shape and cut crosswise, as if cutting rounds. This makes the cube shape.

Serves 2

54 CALORIES PER SERVING: 3 G PROTEIN, 0 G FAT, 11 G CARBOHYDRATE; 21 MG SODIUM; 0 MG CHOLESTEROL

Rooted Carrots

A perfect marriage happens when carrots are combined with other root vegetables. The carrot's sweet flavor complements the strength and robust character of the root vegetables, and its orange pigment adds a warm harvest color to the dish.

1 pound	root vegetables, peeled and cut into chunks (parsnips, rutabagas, or turnips)
2	large carrots, peeled and cut into 1-inch lengths (about ½ pound)
⅛ teaspoon	freshly ground pepper
¹⁄₁₆ teaspoon	ground nutmeg

1. Steam the vegetables until tender. This will take about 20 minutes, less if chopped into small pieces.
2. Mash or puree the vegetables with the spices, adding some of the water used for steaming if a thinner consistency is desired.

Serves 6

67 CALORIES PER SERVING: 1 G PROTEIN, 0 G FAT, 16 G CARBOHYDRATE; 16 MG SODIUM; 0 MG CHOLESTEROL

Baked Acorn Squash Rings

This attractive dish suits any occasion. The round disks with ruffled edges look like flowers, and the golden inner flesh is sweet, tender, and reminiscent of pumpkin.

1	acorn squash (about ½ pound)
1 teaspoon	maple syrup
¼ teaspoon	ground cinnamon
1 teaspoon	water
1	apple, cored and sliced (optional)

1. Wash the squash, then slice it crosswise into ¼-inch rings. Remove the seeds and pulp.
2. Layer the rings in a casserole dish, top with maple syrup, dust on cinnamon, and sprinkle with water. (As an added touch, slices of apple can be placed in layers alternating with the squash rings.)

3. Bake, covered, in a preheated 375 degree F oven for about 30 minutes. The timing and temperature are not critical, so this can bake along with other dinner dishes.

Serves 2

72 CALORIES PER SERVING: 1 G PROTEIN, 0 G FAT, 19 G CARBOHYDRATE;
5 MG SODIUM; 0 MG CHOLESTEROL

Fall Vegetable Medley

I know it is fall when I make this recipe—a colorful, hearty blend of vegetables, each with its own complementary flavor.

½ pound	rutabaga, peeled and cut julienne (about 2 cups)
1	parsnip, peeled and sliced into rounds
1	small zucchini, cut julienne
2	carrots, peeled, cut julienne
1 tablespoon	vegetable oil
	ground pepper to taste

1. Steam the vegetables until just tender, about 10 minutes.
2. Warm the oil in a heavy skillet, but don't allow it to sizzle.
3. Add the vegetables and toss to coat with oil. When the edges of the vegetables start to brown slightly, remove from heat, grind on the pepper, and serve.

Serves 6

64 CALORIES PER SERVING: 1 G PROTEIN, 2 G FAT, 10 G CARBOHYDRATE;
19 MG SODIUM; 0 MG CHOLESTEROL

Vegetables under Wraps

Cooking vegetables wrapped in parchment paper combines the best features of baking and steaming. The vegetables are tenderized in their own juices, and the flavors are intensified by the baking.

1	zucchini, cut into rounds
¼ cup	thinly sliced yellow onion
½	green bell pepper, trimmed and cut into chunks
1	tomato, cut into thick slices
1 cup	quartered mushrooms
½ tablespoon	olive oil
1	bay leaf
	salt and pepper to taste
½ teaspoon	dill seed

1. Cut a piece of parchment paper twice the size of all of the vegetables. Fold it in half, then spread it open. Arrange the vegetables in layers on one side of the paper, beginning with the zucchini, then the onion, bell pepper, tomato, and mushrooms.
2. Drizzle the oil on top and add the bay leaf, salt, pepper, and dill seed.
3. Fold the uncovered half of the parchment over the vegetables, sealing the edges together by making tight folds along the perimeter of the packet. This can be prepared several hours ahead up to this point.
4. Bake in a preheated 375 degree F oven for 45 minutes. Place the whole packet on a serving dish and cut an X into the top, being careful not to be burned by the escaping steam.

Serves 4

35 CALORIES PER SERVING: 1 G PROTEIN, 2 G FAT, 4 G CARBOHYDRATE; 4 MG SODIUM; 0 MG CHOLESTEROL

Potatoes, "Potahtoes," and Spuds

Potatoes are good sources of complex carbohydrates and insoluble fiber, and (without sour cream) are fairly low in calories (only 93 per ⅓ pound). But all potatoes are not created equal, and their differences go well beyond nomenclature. Starch and sugar content, skin thickness, color, and texture vary depending on the type of potato, and these differences greatly affect the flavor and, therefore, the uses of each variety.

Potatoes can be divided into two camps: those that are good boiled, mashed, or steamed and those that are good baked. You can usually tell which is which by sight. The long potatoes are better for baking, and the round ones for cooking with wet heat.

The most basic potato is the all-purpose, or chef, potato. With its thick skin and imperfectly round shape, it is big, coarse, usually dirty, and typically the cheapest spud in the market. Although it has a high starch content, it is low in sugar and moisture, which makes it perfect for thickening a soup or stew, or for making mashed potatoes. It is not good baked.

The Russet potato, also called the Idaho potato (although it is grown in many other states as well), is the typical baking potato, characterized by a smooth oval shape, moderately thick skin, and high moisture content. This is the spud that is baked and served in restaurants. To keep this potato from getting soggy, bake it unwrapped and slit the skin immediately after baking to release the steam.

The red bliss, if sold right after harvest, is considered a new potato. Some white-skinned varieties are also new potatoes. Both the red and white types are best steamed or boiled, and both have thin skins that are good to eat. These potatoes are slightly waxy, with a firm texture, and because they don't fall apart like all-purpose potatoes, they are ideal for salads. Try to buy uniform sizes so the potatoes will cook in the same amount of time.

Recently, more unusual potatoes have been appearing in produce departments. There is a dramatic blue potato, which looks strange to me and tastes okay. I much prefer a yellow spud, sometimes called a yellow finn. This superb potato tastes as though there is butter grown right in it. It is smooth and soft in texture yet holds together for salads and is heavenly when mashed.

You are missing a lot if you use only one kind of potato for every need, for the benefits of using the appropriate spud for a particular dish become abundantly clear right after the first bite.

Confetti Potatoes

Make a large quantity so you'll have leftovers for breakfast. For additional flavor, sauté garlic and onions along with other vegetables.

1 tablespoon	corn oil
5 to 6 cups	cooked potatoes
½	red bell pepper, chopped
½	green bell pepper, chopped
2 tablespoons	chopped fresh parsley
¼ teaspoon	freshly ground pepper
⅛ teaspoon	salt (optional)
dash	paprika for color

1. Heat the oil in a skillet, add the vegetables and parsley, and cook until the potatoes begin to brown.
2. Add salt and pepper, and just prior to serving, dust with paprika.

Serves 6

123 CALORIES PER SERVING: 2 G PROTEIN, 2 G FAT, 24 G CARBOHYDRATE; 6 MG SODIUM; 0 MG CHOLESTEROL

Garlic Lover's Potatoes

This dish is also great cold—right out of the refrigerator—for late-night snacking.

1 pound	new potatoes, the smallest you can find
	olive oil to lightly coat the bottom of a casserole dish (about 1 teaspoon)
4 cloves	garlic, peeled and thickly sliced
1 tablespoon	minced shallot (about ½ bulb)
⅛ teaspoon	salt
	freshly ground pepper to taste
	chopped fresh rosemary or parsley for garnish (optional)

1. Scrub the potatoes well. If large, cut into thick slices. Steam for about 7 minutes, or until they are firm but slightly tender.

2. Pour oil into a casserole dish. Add the steamed potatoes, garlic, shallot, salt, and pepper. Toss to mix well.
3. Bake, uncovered, in a preheated 350 degree F oven for 30 minutes. Stir a couple of times during baking so potatoes cook evenly.
4. If desired, garnish with freshly chopped rosemary or parsley.

Serves 4

106 CALORIES PER SERVING: 3 G PROTEIN, 1 G FAT, 21 G CARBOHYDRATE; 81 MG SODIUM; 0 MG CHOLESTEROL

Dilled New Potatoes

Reheat with low-fat cottage cheese for a satisfying lunch.

1 pound	**new potatoes**
2 teaspoons	**corn oil**
⅛ teaspoon	**salt**
¼ teaspoon	**freshly ground pepper**
1 teaspoon	**minced fresh dill**

1. Cut large potatoes in half and then into thick, even slices. Small potatoes do not have to be cut up, but look quite pretty if a band of skin is peeled away from around the middle.
2. Steam the potatoes until just tender. (At this point they can be refrigerated for as long as a day before finishing the recipe.)
3. Heat the oil in a skillet, add the potatoes, salt, and pepper, and cook, stirring, until the potatoes begin to brown.
4. Toss in the dill, cook for 1 minute longer, and serve.

Serves 4

119 CALORIES PER SERVING: 2 G PROTEIN, 2 G FAT, 23 G CARBOHYDRATE; 69 MG SODIUM; 0 MG CHOLESTEROL

Savory Potatoes

These potatoes darken and intensify as they absorb the soy sauce. Made with stock, they are even heartier fare.

1½ pounds	all-purpose potatoes, peeled and cut into french-fry shapes, or sliced
1	yellow onion, sliced
1 tablespoon	minced fresh parsley
2 tablespoons	soy sauce
⅓ cup	water or stock

1. Toss the ingredients together and place in a covered casserole dish.
2. Bake in a preheated 375 degree F oven for 1½ hours, stirring a couple of times while baking.

Serves 10

67 CALORIES PER SERVING: 2 G PROTEIN, 0 G FAT, 15 G CARBOHYDRATE; 210 MG SODIUM; 0 MG CHOLESTEROL

Sweet Potato Bake

In this country, the words sweet potato and yam are used interchangeably, but there are differences between the two. Sweet potatoes are less sweet, lighter in color, and often drier than yams. Both are better baked in a conventional oven than boiled or microwaved. True yams (botanically speaking) are grown only in South and Central America and are not readily available in the United States.

1 pound	sweet potatoes, peeled and cut into large chunks
1	tart apple, peeled, cored, and sliced
½ teaspoon	grated fresh ginger
¼ teaspoon	ground cinnamon
⅛ teaspoon	ground nutmeg
⅛ to ¼ teaspoon	ground cardamom
1 tablespoon	maple syrup
2 tablespoons	raisins
6	walnuts, halved (optional)
¼ cup	water

1. Steam the sweet potatoes, apple, and ginger until the potato is soft, about 15 minutes.
2. Puree while adding the spices and maple syrup.
3. Pour the mixture into a casserole dish. Top with the raisins and walnuts, arranged in a pattern or just randomly scattered on top.
4. Pour the water over all, but do not stir it in. (It will keep the dish moist while forming a nice top as it bakes.)
5. Bake in a preheated 350 degree F oven for 40 minutes.

Serves 4

227 CALORIES PER SERVING: 3 G PROTEIN, 4 G FAT, 47 G CARBOHYDRATE;
13 MG SODIUM; 0 MG CHOLESTEROL

Lemon Rice

When plain rice seems too bland, but you don't want a heavy, complicated dish, this is a good choice. The lemon zest and parsley lighten both the texture and flavor of the rice. Serve as an accompaniment with fish.

2 cups	water
1 cup	brown rice
2 teaspoons	lemon zest
¼ teaspoon	freshly ground pepper
⅛ teaspoon	salt
1 tablespoon	minced fresh parsley

1. Bring the water to a boil, rinse the rice, and add it to the pot. Cover, reduce heat, and simmer.
2. Add the lemon zest, pepper, and salt to the rice. Cook for 40 minutes, or until all the liquid is absorbed.
3. Just prior to serving, stir in the parsley.

Serves 2

233 CALORIES PER SERVING: 5 G PROTEIN, 1 G FAT, 50 G CARBOHYDRATE;
129 MG SODIUM; 0 MG CHOLESTEROL

South of the Border Rice

Colorful and lightly seasoned, this makes a fine accompaniment for Chili, Bean Enchiladas, or Chicken in a Chili Tomato Sauce (see pages 110, 109, 83).

2 cups	stock or water
1 cup	brown rice
1	yellow onion, chopped (about ½ cup)
1 tablespoon	corn oil
½	green bell pepper, chopped
½ cup	corn kernels, fresh or frozen
½ teaspoon	ground turmeric
dash	hot pepper sauce
⅛ teaspoon	cayenne pepper
¼ teaspoon	salt
1 tablespoon	minced fresh parsley or cilantro

1. Bring the liquid to a boil, rinse the rice, and add it to the pot. Cover, reduce heat, and simmer.
2. Sauté the onion in half of the oil until it is translucent. Pour in the remaining oil, add the bell pepper, and cook until wilted. Stir in the corn kernels (which can be added while still frozen). Add the spices and cook until the onion turns yellow.
3. Add the sautéed vegetables to the pot of simmering rice. Continue to simmer until all of the liquid is absorbed. (Total cooking time should be about 40 minutes.)
4. Stir in the parsley. Remove the pot from the heat, keeping it covered, and let mixture steam for 10 minutes before serving.

Serves 6

124 CALORIES PER SERVING: 2 G PROTEIN, 3 G FAT, 22 G CARBOHYDRATE; 92 MG SODIUM; 0 MG CHOLESTEROL

Raisins and Walnut Pilaf

Quick and easy, with a crunchy texture and subtle sweetness. An ideal choice for those evenings when rice and steamed vegetables are all that's wanted for dinner.

¼ cup	walnut pieces
¼ cup	raisins
¼ cup	water
2 cups	cooked brown rice, preferably short grain

1. In a pan, toast the walnut pieces over dry heat to bring out their flavor. This is an important step.
2. Add the remaining ingredients and cook over low heat, covered, until hot. Shake the pan and stir occasionally to keep the rice from sticking. If freshly cooked, still-warm rice is used, or if reheating in a microwave, omit the water.

Serves 4

191 CALORIES PER SERVING: 4 G PROTEIN, 5 G FAT, 33 G CARBOHYDRATE; 2 MG SODIUM; 0 MG CHOLESTEROL

Dirty Rice

This simple dish can easily serve as a complete meal.

1 clove	garlic, minced (or more for garlic lovers)
1 tablespoon	minced leek
2 tablespoons	pine nuts
1 tablespoon	olive oil
¼ pound	mushrooms, chopped (about 4 large)
2 cups	cooked brown rice
1 tablespoon	minced fresh parsley
1 teaspoon	soy sauce

1. Sauté the garlic, leek, and pine nuts in the olive oil. Add the mushrooms and cook, covered, until they are wilted.
2. Add the brown rice, parsley, and soy sauce. Heat until the rice is warmed through, then serve.

Serves 4

174 CALORIES PER SERVING: 4 G PROTEIN, 6 G FAT, 27 G CARBOHYDRATE; 88 MG SODIUM; 0 MG CHOLESTEROL

Fluffy Kasha

Kasha is a dark brown, earthy, strongly flavored, and nutritious grain. I enjoy it with steamed vegetables for dinner. My great-grandparents cooked kasha with chicken fat and often had the leftovers for breakfast. I leave out the fat and cholesterol, but add egg whites to make it fluffy. If you are in a hurry, simply boil it in water.

1 cup	kasha, cracked or whole
2	egg whites, lightly beaten
2 cups	boiling water

1. Heat a heavy skillet and cook the kasha in the egg whites, stirring constantly.
2. When the egg whites are cooked, pour in the boiling water. (Be careful not to get splattered as the water hits the hot skillet.)
3. Stir the kasha and water, then reduce the heat to low. Cover and cook for 10 minutes if using cracked kasha, 15 if using whole-kernel kasha.
4. With a fork, fluff up the kasha, remove the pot from the heat, cover, and let the mixture steam for 3 minutes before serving.

Serves 6

103 CALORIES PER SERVING: 5 G PROTEIN, 1 G FAT, 22 G CARBOHYDRATE; 17 MG SODIUM; 0 MG CHOLESTEROL

Summertime Couscous

It is important to use fresh herbs in this recipe. Fresh mint can be bought year-round, but home-grown mint is as much a summer necessity for me as is fresh-picked sweet corn. Mint is easy to grow, and will quickly claim a corner of your yard. It also does quite well in pots on a patio or windowsill. You'll always have too much, so use it freely in summertime drinks, in fruit salads, as a garnish, and in bouquets. If fresh chives are unavailable, substitute minced scallions for their flavor, or finely chopped celery for its crunch.

2 cups	cooked couscous (see page 16)
1 clove	garlic, minced
1 teaspoon	olive oil
¼ cup	chopped fresh mint (spearmint is best for cooking)
2 tablespoons	chopped fresh parsley
1 tablespoon	chopped fresh chives
	fresh pepper to taste
½ teaspoon	lemon zest
¼ teaspoon	balsamic vinegar
½ teaspoon	olive oil (optional)

1. Crumble the cooked couscous with a fork or your fingers. (When cooked, it clumps together.)
2. Sauté garlic in 1 teaspoon olive oil over low heat until the garlic turns a light golden color.
3. Add the herbs, pepper, lemon zest, and vinegar. Stir in the couscous and heat through.
4. Use the additional olive oil if you want the dish to be more moist. (This can be prepared ahead and reheated.)

Serves 4

62 CALORIES PER ½ CUP SERVING: 2 G PROTEIN, 1 G FAT, 11 G CARBOHYDRATE; 3 MG SODIUM; 0 MG CHOLESTEROL

Far Eastern Ginger Noodles

Serve with vegetables, tofu cubes, or soup as a main course or as an accompaniment to an entrée. The simple preparation and clear flavors of this dish make it standard fare in my kitchen.

4 ounces	Asian noodles, or ½ pound fresh, such as Chinese flat noodles, udon, soba, or rice (don't substitute Italian pasta)
2 teaspoons	vegetable or sesame oil
2 teaspoons	grated fresh ginger
6	scallions, sliced, using as much of the crisp green tops as possible
2 teaspoons	soy sauce

1. Cook the noodles and drain well. (Rinse with cold water if cooking them well ahead of time.)
2. Heat the oil in a wok or heavy skillet and sauté the ginger until it starts to change color, but don't let it burn. Add the scallions and sauté until wilted.
3. Stir in the noodles and soy sauce, and toss until the noodles are lightly coated.

Serves 2

189 CALORIES PER SERVING: 7 G PROTEIN, 5 G FAT, 32 G CARBOHYDRATE;
359 MG SODIUM; 0 MG CHOLESTEROL

DESSERTS

Desserts come at the end of the meal, when you are no longer hungry, and when you have satisfied most of your nutrient needs. They are the final garnish at the end of the repast; their main role is to make you happy.

Satisfying desserts can be made from wholesome ingredients. They don't need saturated fats, eggs, white sugar, and bleached flour to taste good. To be sure, eliminating ingredients such as butter and cream means that there are some desserts that cannot be included in a low-fat diet—ice cream and flan among them—but there are plenty of other desserts that are well suited to a healthy diet.

Fruit pies, dense cakes, and old-fashioned cookies can all be made with limited fats and sugars. I've included my favorite dessert recipes here. Some even have a decent level of fiber, vitamins, and minerals. But that's not why you should try these recipes. Try them because they are delicious. Try them because they leave you feeling good even after you've eaten one piece too many. Try them because you should be able to have your cake and eat it too.

Fruit Desserts

Fruits, with their naturally high level of sugar, their soft cooked texture, and their lovely colors and variety, lend themselves perfectly to desserts. Of course, fresh, ripe, in-season raw fruits are ideal on their own, but they also excel when dressed up as desserts. Here are some recipes for when they go to town.

Baked Apples

Baked apples lead off this section of fruit desserts because they are familiar and easy to make, and few finales to a meal are as welcoming.

6	baking apples
⅓ cup	raisins
6	cinnamon sticks
½ cup	frozen apple juice concentrate
½ cup	water

¼ teaspoon	ground nutmeg
⅛ teaspoon	ground cloves

1. Wash and core the apples. Set in a baking pan.
2. Put 1 tablespoon of raisins and a cinnamon stick into each apple.
3. Combine the apple juice concentrate and water and pour over the apples. There should be at least ¼ inch of liquid in the bottom of the pan. If not, add water.
4. Dust the tops of the apples with nutmeg and cloves.
5. Bake, covered, in a preheated 375 degree F oven for 30 minutes, or until the apples soften and the skin starts to crack. (A single apple takes 6 minutes in a microwave.)

Serves 6

143 CALORIES PER SERVING: 1 G PROTEIN, 1 G FAT, 37 G CARBOHYDRATE;
8 MG SODIUM; 0 MG CHOLESTEROL

Applesauce

I include this basic recipe as a reminder that the little time it takes to make homemade applesauce is time well spent.

3 pounds	apples, cored and quartered
1 cup	water (less if the apples are fresh, more if old and dry)
1 stick	cinnamon

1. Put the ingredients in a heavy pot, cover, and simmer for 30 minutes.
2. After the apples are cooked, the peels can be picked out and discarded. (I like to leave them in during the cooking for they add a nice color and thicken the sauce.) Or, the peels can be left in and the sauce pureed or run through a food mill. The sauce can also be left chunky, with peels and all.

Serves 5

158 CALORIES PER SERVING: 1 G PROTEIN, 1 G FAT, 42 G CARBOHYDRATE;
0 MG SODIUM; 0 MG CHOLESTEROL

Pears as Blintzes

Blintzes are wonderful crepelike desserts. I used to eat them in delis in New York City when there were still plenty of those classic Jewish Eastern European dairy restaurants in neighborhoods. I took the concept of a blintz and developed this whimsical dessert that uses whole poached pears instead of crepe wrappers to surround a filling. The most familiar blintz is the cheese-filled version, so I use farmer's cheese, a low-fat, soft-curd, fresh cheese with a firmer texture and sweeter flavor than cottage cheese; it is perfect for baking. Serving cheese blintzes with jam is traditional, so I make a sauce from fruit preserves and pour it around the baked pears. Although technically not difficult, this recipe does involve several steps. It is worth the effort, however, for it is an elegant dessert that will delight you when you have time to play in your kitchen.

4 firm pears

Poaching Liquid:

3 cups	water
1 teaspoon	ground cinnamon
½ cup	frozen apple juice concentrate
1 teaspoon	vanilla

Filling:

⅔ cup	farmer's cheese
2 tablespoons	honey
¼ teaspoon	vanilla
1	egg white

Sauce:

1 cup	poaching liquid
1 cup	fruit preserves, preferably fruit juice sweetened
1 tablespoon	arrowroot
1 tablespoon	water

1. Peel the pears and core them all the way through, from top to bottom. Combine the ingredients for the poaching liquid and bring to a simmer. Add the pears and cook over low heat until they soften, about 20-35 minutes, or until a knife can be slipped into the fruit without resistance. Turn the pears over several times while

poaching so that all sides are cooked evenly. When done, remove the pears and discard all but 1 cup of the poaching liquid.

2. Combine the filling ingredients, blending until smooth.

3. Fill the cored pears with the cheese mixture. This is easiest to do with a pastry bag; otherwise, try pushing it in with a knife or small spoon.

4. Set the pears upright in a baking dish. Cover and bake in a preheated 350 degree F oven for 30 minutes.

5. While the pears bake, prepare the sauce by boiling the reserved cup of poaching liquid and the fruit preserves for 5 minutes.

6. In a separate bowl, stir the arrowroot and water into a paste.

7. Turn off the heat under the preserves and, as soon as the liquid stops bubbling, add the arrowroot mixture, stirring until the sauce thickens and clears.

8. Serve the pears, sitting in a pool of sauce, in individual shallow bowls.

Serves 4

436 CALORIES PER SERVING: 9 G PROTEIN, 1 G FAT, 100 G CARBOHYDRATE; 259 MG SODIUM; 3 MG CHOLESTEROL

Poached Pears in Raspberry Sauce

This is colorful, delicious, and surprisingly easy to make. Serve in fancy dessert bowls for an elegant finale.

2 cups	dry red wine
3¼ cups	water
1½ cups	frozen apple juice concentrate
1 slice	fresh ginger
2 sticks	cinnamon
¼ teaspoon	ground nutmeg
6	firm pears, peeled, cored from the bottom, leaving the stem intact
1½ cups	raspberries (fresh or frozen without syrup)
2 tablespoons	arrowroot
	fresh mint and raspberries for garnish (optional)

1. Bring the wine, three cups of the water, and 1 cup of the apple juice concentrate to a boil. Add the ginger, cinnamon, and nutmeg. Reduce the heat to a simmer.
2. Drop in the pears and poach until tender. This will take between 20 and 35 minutes, depending on their ripeness. The pears are done when a knife can be slipped into the fruit without resistance. (Do this from the core end so no marks will show.) If the pears are overcooked, they will fall apart.
3. Remove the pears from the poaching liquid and set onto a serving platter or individual plates.
4. Discard the ginger, cinnamon sticks, and all but 3 cups of the poaching liquid. Add the remaining ½ cup of apple juice concentrate to the poaching liquid and boil until it is reduced to half its original volume (just under 2 cups). This will take less than 15 minutes.
5. Reduce the heat to a simmer and add the raspberries, reserving a few for garnish, if using fresh.
6. In a small bowl, stir together the remaining ¼ cup of water and arrowroot.
7. Remove the reduced poaching liquid from the burner. Slowly add the dissolved arrowroot, stirring constantly until the sauce thickens and clears.
8. Pour the sauce around the pears. Insert a mint leaf near the stem

and place a few fresh whole raspberries in the sauce. Serve warm or chilled.

Serves 6

239 CALORIES PER SERVING: 1 G PROTEIN, 1 G FAT, 47 G CARBOHYDRATE; 63 MG SODIUM; 0 MG CHOLESTEROL

Fruit and Yogurt Frappe

A frappe is a New England word for what is in other areas called a milk shake or a smoothy. This recipe doesn't actually fit the definition of any of those regional specialties. It is cold, sweet, refreshing, and a gorgeous color. For an elegant dessert, it can be used over fruit and presented in chilled crystal stemware, or, for casual fare, it can be poured into a kitchen glass and eaten with a spoon. If made ahead of time and refrigerated, it will have a consistency that is easier to drink.

2	bananas, peeled, broken into chunks, and frozen
⅔ cup	frozen, unsweetened raspberries
⅓ cup	frozen apple juice concentrate
⅓ cup	frozen, unsweetened pineapple juice concentrate
½ teaspoon	lemon juice
2½ cups	low-fat yogurt

1. With a blender or food processor running, drop in the frozen fruit and fruit juices and puree. The frappe will be much thicker if the ingredients are frozen hard before using. (Don't freeze the bananas with their skins on for you'll never be able to peel them.)
2. Add the yogurt and blend until smooth, about 30 seconds.

Serves 4

266 CALORIES PER SERVING: 9 G PROTEIN, 3 G FAT, 54 G CARBOHYDRATE; 107 MG SODIUM; 9 MG CHOLESTEROL

Surprising Strawberries

It is rare to find the smaller, slightly softer, truly ripe, and intensely flavored strawberries in the markets or farm stands. This is unfortunate, for as pretty as those big, red, commercial berries are, they pale in comparison with the old-fashioned varieties. Nevertheless, I still buy strawberries, and they still taste good (though never like those wild berries I remember picking on a hillside in the rain at a summer camp in Vermont). To bring out more flavor, I use an Italian trick: balsamic vinegar. When berries are steeped in this aged, brown liquid, their natural sweetness comes through. In this recipe, I add a touch of maple syrup, too, which creates an unusual but delightful combination.

1 pint	strawberries
1 teaspoon	balsamic vinegar
1 teaspoon	maple syrup
	fresh mint leaves for garnish (optional)

1. Gently wash, then dry the strawberries. Leave on the stems if fresh and green. They make convenient handles for picking up and eating the strawberries later.
2. Arrange the berries on a serving plate.
3. Splash the balsamic vinegar over the berries as evenly as possible, then drizzle with maple syrup, making sure that each one gets a few drops.
4. Let berries sit for at least 1 hour or up to a day before serving.
5. Garnish with mint if desired.

Serves 4

27 CALORIES PER SERVING: 0 G PROTEIN, 0 G FAT, 6 G CARBOHYDRATE; 1 MG SODIUM; 0 MG CHOLESTEROL

Fruit Salad

There are no absolute hard-and-fast rules for making a fruit salad, but there are reasons why some are better than others. Following are suggestions for creating the ultimate fruit salad.

—Always start with a grapefruit. Cut it in half, scoop the segments into a bowl, then squeeze the juice into the bowl. The citrus will prevent other fruits, such as pears and apples, from turning brown. I find this a better solution than dipping them in lemon juice for the grapefruit adds just the right amount of tartness to the salad.

—Do not overuse one type of fruit. Grapes are often added to excess. You really don't need more than 4 types of fruits; otherwise, the salad is so busy you can't appreciate any of them.

—A fruit salad can be made from unusual fruits, such as star fruit, papayas, and mulberries, but this, too, is not necessary. Some of the best salads are made with fresh, local, in-season fruits that have more flavor than many of their imported cousins.

—Certain fruits can be cut a day ahead, while others should be added to the salad just before serving. Here is a guide:

Slice kiwis no more than a couple of hours before use. Ripe kiwis are slightly soft and a bright green color inside; overripe kiwis are dark green and fall apart when sliced; unripened kiwis are hard, light green, and bitter.

Melons, pears, apples, blueberries, oranges, papayas, and pineapple can all be cut and mixed a day ahead of time.

Strawberries, raspberries, blackberries, and bananas should be added shortly before serving.

—The ideal fruit salad is as beautiful as it is flavorful. Select fruits according to how they will look together. Think about the shape of the pieces, too. Use a melon baller. Cut fruits into a uniform size. Serve in a pretty bowl or in a basket carved out of a melon. Garnish with fresh mint, twists of orange, or a few of the nicest berries.

— Texture is also important. For example, combine the crunch of an apple with the softness of a ripe melon.

Dessert Fruit Plates

You can make individual dessert plates that look like works of art by designing arrangements of exotic fruits, such as papayas, kiwis, and carambola, in pools of Yogurt and Mint Sauce (see following recipe). What follows is a suggestion to get you started.

1	papaya
1	kiwi
½ pint	blueberries
½ pint	raspberries
1 cup	Yogurt and Mint Sauce
	(see following recipe)
	fresh mint for garnish (optional)

1. Peel the papaya and scoop out the seeds, discarding them. Cut the fruit into long thin slices.
2. Peel the kiwi and slice into rounds.
3. Gently wash the blueberries. Avoid washing the raspberries if possible, since they easily turn into mush.
4. Arrange the fruit on 6 dessert plates.
5. Pour the sauce over the fruit in a narrow stream so there is a little on each type of fruit, but none is completely covered by the sauce. Garnish with mint if desired.

Serves 6

80 CALORIES PER SERVING: 3 G PROTEIN, 1 G FAT, 17 G CARBOHYDRATE; 30 MG SODIUM; 2 MG CHOLESTEROL (see following recipe for sauce analysis)

Fruit Salad with Yogurt and Mint Sauce

A simple fruit salad enhanced with a cool and refreshing sauce.

1	grapefruit
1	melon (about 2 1/2 pounds), scooped into balls
1	orange, segments removed from the membranes
1 pint	berries

Yogurt and Mint Sauce:

2 cups	low-fat yogurt
2 tablespoons	minced fresh mint
¼ teaspoon	vanilla
1 tablespoon	honey

1. Cut the grapefruit in half and scoop out the segments. Put the segments into a bowl. Squeeze the juice from the grapefruit into the bowl.
2. Add the 3 remaining fruits, toss, and chill.
3. Whisk together all of the sauce ingredients, combine with the chilled fruit, and serve.

Serves 8

FRUIT SALAD
61 CALORIES PER SERVING: 1 G PROTEIN, 1 G FAT, 15 G CARBOHYDRATE;
8 MG SODIUM; 0 MG CHOLESTEROL

YOGURT AND MINT SAUCE
44 CALORIES PER SERVING: 3 G PROTEIN, 1 G FAT, 6 G CARBOHYDRATE;
40 MG SODIUM; 4 MG CHOLESTEROL

Cakes and Dessert Squares

It is possible to make some wonderful low-fat cakes and dessert squares, but it is not possible to make *every* cake or square low in fat. Pound cake is not the same without that pound of butter, and brownies aren't brownies if they're not rich and sinful. Also, since I avoid using white sugar, it is difficult to achieve a light yellow cake; honey and other alternative sweeteners make dense, moist confections, not airy ones.

In spite of it all, excellent cakes and squares can be made using whole wheat flour, natural sweeteners, and only a little oil. These are desserts that you expect to be dark, moist, and flavorful. And they are every bit as good (if not better) than their richer relatives.

Current Currant Carrot Cake

Moist and sweet, this cake can be iced with "Marshmallow Fluff" (recipe follows) or left ungarnished (easier to pack for bag lunches). Instead of raisins, I use currants, which are not related to raisins at all. They are the dried fruit of a shrub that is grown in European countries, especially France and England. I like their small size and sweet flavor. Most markets stock them next to the raisins.

1½ cups	whole wheat pastry flour
1½ cups	unbleached white flour
2 teaspoons	baking soda
2 teaspoons	ground cinnamon
¾ teaspoon	ground nutmeg
¼ teaspoon	ground cloves
¼ teaspoon	salt
4	egg whites
⅔ cup	vegetable oil
⅔ cup	buttermilk
1¼ cups	honey
2 cups	shredded carrots (about 3 to 4 carrots)
8-ounce can	crushed pineapple, packed in its own natural juice, well drained
1 cup	currants

1. Grease a 10-inch bundt pan. (A bundt pan is essential for baking moist batters such as this one, for the tube in the center assures that the cake will cook evenly. Without it, the cake would start to burn before the inside was done.)
2. Sift together the dry ingredients.
3. In a separate, large bowl, beat the egg whites and oil. Whisk in the buttermilk, then slowly add the honey, and beat until creamy.
4. Stir the carrots, pineapple, and currants into the wet ingredients.
5. Add the dry ingredients to the wet and stir gently until the batter is mixed but not totally smooth. (If overmixed, the cake will be tough.)
6. Pour the batter into the bundt pan. Tap the pan on the table to remove air pockets and smooth out the top.
7. Bake the cake in a preheated 375 degree F oven for 1 hour. If your oven doesn't heat evenly, the cake must be turned several times while baking. Opening the oven door will not hurt it unless the door is slammed shut; however, each time the door is opened, the oven temperature will drop and the cooking time will have to be extended.

8. The cake is done when it feels firm to the touch.
9. Cool on a wire rack for 10 minutes before removing it from the bundt pan, and then invert the cake onto a wire rack. Transfer to a cake plate only after it is thoroughly cooled or the bottom will become soggy.

Serves 12

384 CALORIES PER SERVING: 6 G PROTEIN, 13 G FAT, 66 G CARBOHYDRATE;
222 MG SODIUM; 1 MG CHOLESTEROL

"Marshmallow Fluff"

This is a light, sweet, white icing that reminds me of a childhood favorite of the same name. It is cooked in a double boiler, but you can construct your own using a pot and a stainless steel bowl sitting on top. The use of a bowl makes mixing easier.

1	egg white
¼ cup	honey
½ teaspoon	vanilla
pinch	salt

1. Bring water to a boil in the bottom of a double boiler. The water should not touch the bottom of the bowl or pan set on top.
2. Put the ingredients into the bowl. Place over the boiling water and beat with an electric mixer for 2 minutes, until the egg whites expand and thicken to soft peaks. (Be careful not to overbeat to the stiff-peak stage, for this results in a dense frosting.)
3. Remove bowl from the double boiler and continue to beat frosting until cool.

Makes enough for a bundt or 9-inch by 12-inch cake serving 12

46 CALORIES PER SERVING: 1 G PROTEIN, 0 G FAT, 12 G CARBOHYDRATE;
30 MG SODIUM; 0 MG CHOLESTEROL

Chocolate

I couldn't write the dessert chapter without a chocolate recipe. I love chocolate, but try to be sane about how much I eat. Because the average chocolate dessert, whether a candy bar or a brownie, contains large quantities of ingredients that I don't usually consume, such as butter and white sugar, as well as artificial flavorings and cheap fats, it is not hard to pass it by. But when the dessert is made from scratch by a talented pastry chef using high-quality ingredients and imagination, I indulge.

It's not just the butter in that Black Forest Cake that contributes fat calories to a dessert recipe. Pure baking chocolate also contains fat, in the form of cocoa butter. The fat in chocolate gives it its smooth, silky, melt-in-your-mouth texture. Cocoa is chocolate with much of the cocoa butter removed (it has up to ⅔ less than baking chocolate), so, I bake with cocoa.

Besides the fat, chocolate has some other nutritional drawbacks, such as caffeine. But, on its own, chocolate isn't that bad, and when used in a recipe that has reduced sugar, some whole wheat flour, and no cholesterol, I figure that I can eat it and not feel guilty.

Cocoa Cake

This sheet cake is easy to make. I bake it on those nights when I absolutely must have a dessert before going to bed. What isn't eaten in the first 24 hours is cut into squares, wrapped in plastic, and frozen.

½ cup	dry sweetener (date, maple, cane)
2 teaspoons	coffee substitute (such as Postum or Cafix) dissolved in ⅔ cup hot water
½ cup	vegetable oil
1½ cups	honey
¾ cup	buttermilk
¾ cup	cocoa
1½ teaspoons	baking soda
1 teaspoon	baking powder
1 cup	whole wheat pastry flour
1 cup	unbleached white flour
3	egg whites, beaten to a soft peak

1. Dissolve the dry sweetener in the hot coffee substitute. Add the oil and the honey and combine. (By measuring the oil first, the cup is greased and the honey will slip right out, which solves one of those kitchen frustrations of sticky honey stuck in the measuring cup.) Whisk in the buttermilk.
2. Sift the dry ingredients together in the order shown.
3. Fold the wet ingredients into the dry using a rubber spatula. The cocoa resists incorporation into the liquid and tends to float in dry lumps, but don't beat it. Stir briskly in a circular motion, then slowly fold the batter over and over until moist and almost, but not entirely, smooth. Fold in the egg whites until only thin white streaks show.
4. Pour the batter into a greased 9-inch by 12-inch baking pan.
5. Bake in a preheated 350 degree F oven for about 45 minutes. Take care not to overcook the batter. The cake is done when it feels firm in the center, and a toothpick comes out a bit moist but not coated.

Serves 12

366 CALORIES PER SERVING: 7 G PROTEIN, 11 G FAT, 63 G CARBOHYDRATE; 200 MG SODIUM; 1 MG CHOLESTEROL

Fudge Glaze

Be sure the cake and the glaze have cooled sufficiently before spreading.

⅓ cup	honey
½ cup	low-fat milk
¼ cup	cocoa
½ teaspoon	vanilla

1. Combine all the ingredients in a blender or food processor fitted with metal blade. Mix until smooth, scraping down the sides of the bowl once or twice.
2. Transfer to a heavy saucepan and cook over medium-high heat, whisking until it starts to boil. Reduce heat to medium and cook for 10–15 minutes or until slightly thickened, whisking constantly.
3. Let the glaze cool, then drizzle over the cooled cake.

Makes enough for a 9-inch by 12-inch cake serving 12

41 CALORIES PER SERVING: 1 G PROTEIN, 0 G FAT, 9 G CARBOHYDRATE; 7 MG SODIUM; 1 MG CHOLESTEROL

Gingerbread

Dark brown, spicy, and delicious—an old-fashioned favorite. This recipe received the ultimate compliment from a friend who said that it reminded him of summer vacations to the country when he was young.

¼ cup	honey
⅔ cup	molasses
⅓ cup	vegetable oil
1½ cups	low-fat milk
1½ cups	whole wheat pastry flour
⅔ cup	unbleached white flour
¼ teaspoon	baking soda
1½ teaspoons	baking powder
1 tablespoon	ground cinnamon
2 teaspoons	ground ginger
¼ teaspoon	ground cloves
2	egg whites, beaten to a soft peak

1. Whisk together the honey, molasses, oil, and milk. If the honey and molasses are too firm to mix, warm them first.
2. Sift together the dry ingredients.
3. Form a well in the center of the dry mixture and pour in the wet. Fold with a spatula until the batter is moist but still lumpy. Gently fold in the egg whites. This will be a thin batter.
4. Pour into a nonstick or greased 9-inch square pan.
5. Bake in a preheated 375 degree F oven for 1 hour or until it feels firm to the touch.

Serves 10

193 CALORIES PER SERVING: 5 G PROTEIN, 7 G FAT, 28 G CARBOHYDRATE; 100 MG SODIUM; 2 MG CHOLESTEROL

Jam Squares

Enjoy these at breakfast, topped with low-fat yogurt, or late in the afternoon with a mug of tea.

½ cup	honey
½ cup	malt syrup
¾ cup	buttermilk
½ cup	vegetable oil
2	egg whites
1¾ cups	whole wheat pastry flour
1 teaspoon	ground cinnamon
¼ teaspoon	salt
½ teaspoon	baking soda
2 cups	rolled oats
¾ cup	fruit preserves, any flavor sweetened with fruit juices

1. Warm the honey and malt syrup until they are pourable. Do this in the microwave or in a pyrex dish over boiling water.
2. Whisk together the buttermilk, oil, and egg whites, then whisk in the warmed sweeteners.
3. Sift together the flour, cinnamon, salt, and baking soda. Add the oats and stir to combine.
4. Stir the wet and dry mixtures together.
5. Spread half of the batter in a nonstick or greased 9-inch square pan. Distribute the preserves evenly on top. Pour the rest of the batter into the pan and spread evenly.
6. Bake in a preheated 400 degree F oven for 50-60 minutes.

Serves 10

342 CALORIES PER SERVING: 7 G PROTEIN, 13 G FAT, 55 G CARBOHYDRATE; 126 MG SODIUM; 1 MG CHOLESTEROL

Greasing the Pan

I am much too attached to my old, dark, seasoned pans and my heavy-weight stainless ones to give them up for nonstick varieties, so there are times when my pans have to be greased. Nonstick sprays are good choices for cookie sheets and cake pans, but buy the simple, unflavored brands; ''butter flavored'' means pure chemicals, and tastes it.

Don't grease pans with vegetable oil, which will burn and scorch before cookies and cakes have time to brown.

For muffin tins, I use soy margarine. I haven't been able to find a margarine in a supermarket that doesn't rely on artificial colorings and flavorings, so I buy from the natural food store. Because margarine is more saturated than oil, it softens rather than hardens the outsides of baked goods.

I use parchment paper on cookie sheets and springform pans. Unlike wax paper, it doesn't leave any residue on the food. I also use it when rolling out pie shells. Note that because parchment paper is white and reflects heat, food won't brown as quickly when it is used. The medium-weight commercial sheets used by bakeries are the best parchment. See if your neighborhood bakery will sell you some.

Cookies

◆

Cookies are a universal favorite, and when made with healthful ingredients, they can be eaten anytime. In fact, I frequently eat oatmeal cookies for breakfast. I think of them as hot cereal in another form.

Because there is no butter and only a small amount of oil in the following recipes, these cookies don't leave me feeling stuffed and lethargic. They tend to go stale fast, so I freeze them soon after they are baked and warm a handful at a time in my microwave, which takes less than 45 seconds. They taste freshly baked.

Oatmeal Drop Cookies

Spicy, sweet, and chewy, these cookies are simple to make and easy to eat.

¼ cup	low-fat yogurt
¼ cup	vegetable oil
½ cup	maple syrup or honey
1 cup	rolled oats
½ cup	whole wheat pastry flour
1 teaspoon	baking powder
1 tablespoon	ground cinnamon
½ cup	raisins
½ cup	chopped walnuts (apples can be substituted)

1. Stir together the yogurt, oil, and sweetener, then mix in the oats.
2. Sift the flour, baking powder, and cinnamon over the wet ingredients, add the raisins and walnuts, and stir until mixed.
3. Drop tablespoonsful of the batter onto a greased or nonstick cookie sheet, or one lined with parchment paper.
4. Bake in a preheated 375 degree F oven for about 25 minutes or until light brown.

Yields about 20 cookies

108 CALORIES PER COOKIE: 2 G PROTEIN, 5 G FAT, 15 G CARBOHYDRATE; 20 MG SODIUM; 0 MG CHOLESTEROL

Spicy Applesauce Cookies

A wholesome, hearty treat to keep on hand for lunches as well as for midday or midnight snacking.

½ cup	vegetable oil
1 cup	thick applesauce, preferably homemade (see page 147)
½ teaspoon	vanilla
¾ cup	whole wheat pastry flour
¼ teaspoon	ground cloves
¼ teaspoon	ground nutmeg
½ teaspoon	ground cinnamon
½ cup	dry sweetener (date, maple, cane)
¼ cup	chopped nuts
2 cups	rolled oats
¼ cup	raisins

1. Mix the oil, applesauce, and vanilla together.
2. Sift the flour and spices into a separate bowl. Stir in the sweetener, nuts, oats, and raisins.
3. Combine the wet and dry ingredients, stirring until there are no dry lumps.
4. Drop tablespoonsful of the batter onto a greased or nonstick cookie sheet, or one lined with parchment paper.
5. Bake in a preheated 375 degree F oven for about 25 minutes, or until the cookies turn light brown. Cool on a rack. (Remember that cookies baked on parchment will take longer to bake. Cookies on a greased sheet may brown too quickly on their bottoms; lower the oven temperature by 25 degrees if this starts to happen.)

Yields 2½ dozen

89 CALORIES PER COOKIE: 2 G PROTEIN, 5 G FAT, 11 G CARBOHYDRATE; 1 MG SODIUM; 0 MG CHOLESTEROL

Cookies!

The types of cookies that can spring from this basic mix are infinite. I
have included two variations to get you started.

½ cup	low-fat yogurt
⅓ cup	vegetable oil
½ cup	honey
2	egg whites
½ teaspoon	vanilla
1 teaspoon	baking powder
1 cup	whole wheat pastry flour
2 to 3 cups	imagination—(at least 1½ cups should be semi-liquid, like grated apples, carrots, or mashed bananas)

Variation 1:

1½ cups	grated carrots
½ cup	raisins
⅔ cup	rolled oats
1 teaspoon	ground cinnamon

Variation 2:

½ cup	chopped dates
1½ cups	grated apple
¼ cup	oat or wheat bran

1. Whisk together the wet ingredients.
2. In separate bowl, sift together the dry and stir in the cups of
   imagination.
3. Fold in the wet ingredients until everything is moist.
4. Drop tablespoonsful of the batter onto a greased or nonstick cookie
   sheet, or one lined with parchment paper.
5. Bake in a preheated 375 degree F oven for about 25 minutes, or
   until done.

Yields 1½ dozen

102 CALORIES PER COOKIE: 2 G PROTEIN, 4 G FAT, 15 G CARBOHYDRATE;
30 MG SODIUM; 1 MG CHOLESTEROL (analysis used mashed bananas)

Almond Loves

A great holiday cookie—fancy-looking, easy to make, with a marzipanlike flavor. Although free of cholesterol, they are very rich.

1¾ cups	almonds
2	egg whites
⅓ cup	honey
1 tablespoon	vegetable oil
¼ teaspoon	ground nutmeg
¼ teaspoon	ground cardamom
¼ cup	fruit preserves, preferably sweetened with juice or honey

1. In a food processor fitted with metal blade or in a blender, grind together everything except the preserves until a smooth paste forms.
2. Drop teaspoonsful of the paste onto a greased or nonstick cookie sheet, or one lined with parchment paper. With a wet spoon, make a depression in the centers of the cookies.
3. Place a small dollop (about ½ teaspoon) of fruit preserves in each depression.
4. Bake in a preheated 350 degree F oven until lightly golden, between 10–15 minutes.

Yields 2½ dozen

64 CALORIES PER COOKIE: 2 G PROTEIN, 4 G FAT, 6 G CARBOHYDRATE; 5 MG SODIUM; 0 MG CHOLESTEROL

Pies

I live 5 minutes from commercial orchards and berry farms, so by the first week that the farm stands have local produce, I've made at least one pie. All summer there are berries, rhubarb, and peaches, and in the fall—apples.

Because I have fresh apples of many varieties close at hand, each pie I make is different from the next. The one filled with sour

Gravensteins and sweet Paula Reds will always stay fondly in my memory. Everyone has his or her own personal favorites, so use the types and combinations you prefer.

Making Pie Crust

Pie crusts are tricky, and oil crusts made with whole wheat pastry flour are the hardest to get right. But, they are worth the effort. Whole wheat pastry flour gives the crust a nutty flavor, and the oil creates the flaky texture of the butter and lard versions, but without the cholesterol and saturated fat.

One problem with whole wheat pastry flour is that it absorbs less liquid than white flour, and thus it tends to crumble instead of roll out smoothly. Consequently, I use only ½ cup whole wheat flour. If you've never made a crust before, use only white flour until you get a feel for it. (Adjust the recipe by using 1 more tablespoon of water.) Another difficulty is that whole wheat flours vary, and what works once may not work exactly the same way the next time.

I don't mean to discourage you from making pie crusts, but simply want to warn you that those first efforts might not be quite what you had hoped for. Good crusts do take practice, but eventually they become very easy to make.

Pay close attention to your dough and handle it carefully. Start with chilled ingredients. Measure the oil and water in separate containers and put them in the freezer for a few minutes.

Tough doughs are caused by overworking. Avoid this by quickly stirring the oil into the flour with a fork. The dough will ball up into small clumps. Next, add the water, a tablespoon at a time. The more water, the easier the dough will be to roll out, but too much water toughens the dough. Add enough to form a soft, silky ball with two to three motions of your hand.

Wrap the dough in plastic and chill in the refrigerator for 15 minutes. This allows the moisture to spread evenly throughout the dough, and the chilling makes it easier to roll out.

Roll the dough between sheets of parchment or wax paper. The paper keeps the dough from sticking to the board and rolling pin; it also makes it easier to place in the pie plate. Remove the top sheet of paper, then, with the crust still stuck to the other sheet, center it over the pie plate, press in position, and peel off the paper.

I like fluted edges around my pies. To achieve this, trim the crust so there is an even amount around the rim of the pie plate. When the top crust is set on the pie, trim that, too, so that the edges meet with a little to spare. Press the upper and lower crusts together. They can be sealed with the tines of a fork, which makes pretty lines around the pie, or fluted by pushing the crust with the tip of the forefinger of one hand into a V formed by the thumb and forefinger of the other hand.

Excess pie crust can be rolled out, cut into hearts or other shapes, and pressed onto the top of the pie. I also like to cut a vent in the shape of a star.

For a nicely browned crust, combine 2 teaspoons skim milk with 1 teaspoon dry sweetener and brush on the top crust just prior to baking.

Pie Crust

Most pie crusts are made with up to ½ cup butter or solid shortening. Those saturated fats make the crust tender but also high in calories and cholesterol. It is impossible to make a crust without some sort of fat, which is why many low-fat cookbooks use a pat-in cereal crust bearing no resemblance to the real thing. The recipe I offer here uses polyunsaturated oil, some whole wheat flour, and reduced salt. This is a compromise between the purists and the realists, but there is little compromise in flavor or texture.

1¾ cups	unbleached white flour
½ cup	whole wheat pastry flour
½ teaspoon	salt
9 tablespoons	oil
3 to 4 tablespoons	cold water

1. Before beginning, please read Making Pie Crust on page 167.
2. Sift the flours and salt together and stir to blend.
3. Make a well in the center and pour in the oil, mixing all the while with a fork. Do this quickly until moist clumps of dough form.
4. While mixing with the fork, add the water, a tablespoon at a time, until the dough forms a ball.
5. Shape the ball with your hands. Knead about 3 times, using quick, light motions.
6. Divide the dough in half, wrap each half in plastic, and chill for 15 minutes.
7. Place dough on a lightly floured surface or between two sheets of parchment or wax paper. Working from the center outward, roll out the dough. With each stroke, change the direction you are pushing the rolling pin so that a circle is formed.

8. Repeat the procedure for other half of dough, then proceed with pie recipe.

Yields two 9-inch pie crusts

173 CALORIES PER SERVING: 3 G PROTEIN, 10 G FAT, 17 G CARBOHYDRATE; 89 MG SODIUM; 0 MG CHOLESTEROL

Peach Pie

This is a summertime pie—it relies on ripe fruit. Hard peaches, even if they look ripe, have no flavor and will make a boring pie. Sometimes they never ripen, but just get soft and mealy. Ripe peaches feel juicy to the touch, but shouldn't be pressed too much because they are prone to bruises. You'll know that you picked the right peaches if, on the way home from the market, the smell of ripe fruit fills your car.

10	freestone peaches
⅓ cup	maple syrup
1½ tablespoons	arrowroot
	Pie Crust (see page 168)

1. Drop the peaches in a pot of boiling water for 15 seconds. Remove immediately, cool, and peel. Cut in half and remove the pits, then cut halves in half. (There will be about 5 cups of fruit.)
2. Combine the peaches with the maple syrup and arrowroot.
3. Set the bottom crust in a pie plate and prick the bottom. Pour filling into the pie crust.
4. Place the upper crust on the pie and flute the edges, or seal them with the tines of a fork. Cut steam vents in the top crust.
5. Bake in a preheated 425 degree F oven for 20 minutes, then reduce to 350 and bake for 30–40 minutes longer, or until the crust browns.

Serves 12

230 CALORIES PER SERVING: 3 G PROTEIN, 10 G FAT, 32 G CARBOHYDRATE; 91 MG SODIUM; 0 MG CHOLESTEROL

Traditional Apple Pie

The nice thing about this recipe is that you aren't aware of the alternative sugars. The flavor simply is sweetened apples—traditional, homey, and comforting.

6	baking apples
1 teaspoon	lemon juice
1½ tablespoons	arrowroot
¼ teaspoon	ground nutmeg
½ tablespoon	ground cinnamon
½ cup	frozen apple juice concentrate (less if the apples are a sweet variety)
¼ cup	malt or maple syrup
	Pie Crust (see page 168)

1. Peel and core the apples. Slice into fairly large wedges and toss with the lemon juice to prevent browning.
2. Add the arrowroot, nutmeg, and cinnamon to the apples. Toss until the apples are well coated.
3. Pour in the apple juice concentrate and syrup. Stir until all ingredients are mixed well.
4. Place the bottom crust in a pie plate. Press down and trim the edges. Fill the crust with the apples, piling them highest in the center.
5. Top the pie with the upper crust and crimp the two crusts together. Slice steam vents in the top, or cut one out of the center in the shape of a star.
6. Bake in a preheated 425 degree F oven for 20 minutes, then reduce to 375 and bake for another 30 minutes.

Serves 12

242 CALORIES PER SERVING: 3 G PROTEIN, 11 G FAT, 35 G CARBOHYDRATE; 93 MG SODIUM; 0 MG CHOLESTEROL

More Than Apple Pie

You don't have to buy fancy fruit for pie. It can have scabs and be oddly shaped. As long as it isn't bruised, it'll do fine.

6	baking apples (about 1½ pounds)
½ tablespoon	lemon juice
¼ cup	honey
1 teaspoon	ground cinnamon
⅛ teaspoon	ground cloves
⅓ cup	walnuts
⅓ cup	raisins
	Pie Crust (see page 168)

1. Peel, core, and slice the apples. Toss with the lemon juice to prevent browning and to enhance flavor.
2. Combine with the honey, spices, walnuts, and raisins.
3. Place the bottom crust in a pie plate. Pour the apple mixture into the pie shell, mounding it in the center.
4. Place the upper crust on top and pinch the edges of the crusts together. Cut steam vents in the top. (I like to make a star shape.)
5. Bake in a preheated 425 degree F oven for 20 minutes or until the crust starts to brown. Reduce the heat to 375 and bake for 30 minutes longer.

Serves 12

262 CALORIES PER SERVING: 4 G PROTEIN, 13 G FAT, 36 G CARBOHYDRATE; 91 MG SODIUM; 0 MG CHOLESTEROL

Pumpkin Pie

Even after an abundant Thanksgiving dinner, this pumpkin pie is always welcome. It has all the flavor and texture of its richer cousin, but none of the heavy fats and creams. If you're especially concerned about fats, bake the filling in custard dishes. Without the pie crust it has less than 1 gram of fat per serving.

2 cups	pureed pumpkin, or 15-ounce can
¾ cup	pureed cottage cheese
⅓ cup	evaporated skim milk
⅓ cup	maple syrup
½ cup	malt syrup
1 teaspoon	ground cinnamon
¼ teaspoon	ground ginger
⅛ teaspoon	ground cloves
⅛ teaspoon	allspice
1½ tablespoons	arrowroot
2	egg whites, beaten to a soft peak
	Pie Crust (use half the recipe on page 168)

1. Combine all but the egg whites in a food processor fitted with metal blade. Transfer to a bowl and fold in egg whites.
2. Place the single crust in a pie plate and pour in the batter.
3. Bake in a preheated 425 degree F oven for 15 minutes, then reduce to 350 and bake for about 1 hour. The pie is done when a knife inserted into the center comes out clean.

Serves 12

186 CALORIES PER SERVING: 5 G PROTEIN, 6 G FAT, 30 G CARBOHYDRATE; 159 MG SODIUM; 1 MG CHOLESTEROL

QUICK BREADS

You'll notice that this section has an inordinate number of selections. I love quick breads. Often when I'm hungry for something in the evening, I'll make a batch of muffins and satisfy my craving without resorting to junk food. Muffins are best if eaten within 24 hours of baking because they stay fresh for such a short period of time. But even I can't eat a dozen muffins in a day, so I freeze most of them. When I want one, I just pop a frozen muffin in the microwave, and in less than a minute get fresh-baked taste and texture.

Biscuits are also one of my favorites. It is extremely satisfying to work with the dough, shape the biscuits by hand, and watch them cook—all in less than an hour.

Cranberry Maple Muffins

This recipe is a tribute to two of my favorite New England foods: cranberries and maple syrup. These classic ingredients create an exceptional muffin.

2 cups	whole wheat pastry flour
1 teaspoon	baking soda
¼ teaspoon	salt
1 cup	buttermilk
2	egg whites
¼ cup	maple syrup
¼ cup	vegetable oil
2 tablespoons	honey
1 cup	cranberries, sorted and rinsed

1. Sift together the flour, baking soda, and salt.
2. In another bowl, whisk the buttermilk, egg whites, maple syrup, oil, and honey.
3. Form a well in the center of the dry ingredients and pour in the wet. Fold until batter is moistened but still lumpy. Fold in the cranberries. (If frozen, they do not have to be defrosted.)
4. Pour into greased muffin tins and bake in a preheated 350 degree F oven for 25–30 minutes, or until lightly brown on top.

Yields 1 dozen

132 CALORIES PER MUFFIN: 4 G PROTEIN, 5 G FAT, 19 G CARBOHYDRATE;
143 MG SODIUM; 1 MG CHOLESTEROL

Apple Muffins

Plump, moist, and spicy-sweet, these are satisfying anytime of day—hot from the oven for breakfast, as an accompaniment to a fruit salad for lunch, or mid-afternoon with a cup of hot tea.

2 cups	whole wheat pastry flour
½ cup	unbleached white flour
1 teaspoon	ground cinnamon
⅛ teaspoon	allspice
1½ teaspoons	baking soda
½ teaspoon	baking powder
2	egg whites
1 cup	buttermilk
¼ cup	vegetable oil
½ cup	honey
2	apples, peeled and grated (about 1½ cups)

1. Sift together the dry ingredients.
2. In another bowl, beat the egg whites, buttermilk, oil, and honey until creamy. Stir in the apples.
3. Form a well in the center of the dry ingredients and pour in the wet mixture. Fold together until moistened. The batter can be lumpy, but there shouldn't be any dry patches of flour.
4. Pour into greased muffin tins and bake in a preheated 350 degree F oven for 25–30 minutes.

Yields 1 dozen

195 CALORIES PER MUFFIN: 5 G PROTEIN, 5 G FAT, 35 G CARBOHYDRATE; 149 MG SODIUM; 1 MG CHOLESTEROL

Corn Muffins

For a change of pace, serve these corn muffins instead of traditional rolls at your next dinner party.

½ cup	whole wheat pastry flour
1½ cups	unbleached white flour
1 cup	cornmeal (not degerminated, see page 179)
1 tablespoon	baking powder
¼ teaspoon	salt
⅓ cup	vegetable oil
1½ cups	low-fat milk
2 tablespoons	molasses
¼ cup	honey
1	egg white, beaten

1. Sift together the dry ingredients.
2. In a separate bowl, whisk together the oil, milk, and sweeteners.
3. Make a well in the center of the dry ingredients and pour in the wet mixture. Fold with a rubber spatula until moistened. Fold in the egg white.
4. Pour into greased muffin tins and bake in preheated 350 degree F oven for 25–30 minutes or until the edges just start to brown.

Yields 1 dozen

207 CALORIES PER MUFFIN: 5 G PROTEIN, 7 G FAT, 32 G CARBOHYDRATE; 148 MG SODIUM; 1 MG CHOLESTEROL

Blueberry Buttermilk Muffins

Serve these 100% whole wheat muffins for a country brunch.

2 cups	whole wheat pastry flour
1 teaspoon	baking soda
1¼ cups	buttermilk
2	egg whites, lightly beaten
½ cup	honey
⅓ cup	vegetable oil
1 cup	blueberries, fresh or frozen

1. Sift the flour and baking soda together.

2. In a separate bowl, whisk the next 4 ingredients together until creamy, then stir in the blueberries.
3. Form a well in the center of the dry ingredients and pour in the wet. Fold together until the batter is moistened yet slightly lumpy.
4. Pour into greased muffin tins and bake in a preheated 350 degree F oven for 25–30 minutes.

Yields 1 dozen

182 CALORIES PER MUFFIN: 4 G PROTEIN, 7 G FAT, 29 G CARBOHYDRATE; 105 MG SODIUM; 1 MG CHOLESTEROL

Berry-Good Muffins

Use any berry you want in this recipe, either fresh or frozen. Frozen berries do not have to be thawed, but they will chill the batter, so add an extra minute or two to the cooking time.

1	egg white
1 cup	low-fat yogurt
¼ cup	oil
¼ teaspoon	vanilla
¼ cup	maple syrup or honey
1 cup	whole wheat pastry flour
1 cup	unbleached white flour
¼ cup	dry sweetener (maple, cane, date)
¼ teaspoon	salt
½ teaspoon	baking soda
1½ teaspoons	baking powder
1½ cups	berries

1. Whisk together the egg white, yogurt, oil, vanilla, and maple syrup.
2. In a separate bowl, sift together the flours, dry sweetener, salt, baking soda, and baking powder.
3. Form a well in the center of the dry ingredients. Pour in the wet ingredients and fold together with a spatula until moist but still slightly lumpy. Fold in the berries.
4. Pour into greased muffin tins and bake in a preheated 350 degree F oven for about 30 minutes.

Yields 1 dozen

173 CALORIES PER MUFFIN: 4 G PROTEIN, 5 G FAT, 29 G CARBOHYDRATE; 138 MG SODIUM; 1 MG CHOLESTEROL

Honey Banana Muffins

Tender and moist, with a sweet banana flavor, these muffins disprove the theory that it is impossible to make a light, low-fat, whole wheat muffin. Be sure to use ripe bananas—the riper, the sweeter, the better.

1 cup	unbleached white flour
2 cups	whole wheat pastry flour
2 teaspoons	baking soda
¼ teaspoon	salt
¼ teaspoon	ground nutmeg
⅔ cup	honey
1⅓ cups	buttermilk
⅓ cup	vegetable oil
3	egg whites, beaten to a soft peak
2	ripe bananas, mashed (about 1 cup)

1. Sift together the dry ingredients.
2. In a separate bowl, whisk together the honey, buttermilk, and oil. Gently stir in the egg whites.
3. Combine the bananas with the wet ingredients.
4. Form a well in the center of the dry ingredients and pour in the wet. Fold together until the batter is moist but still lumpy.
5. Pour into greased muffin tins and bake in a preheated 350 degree F oven for 25–30 minutes.

Yields 1½ dozen

161 CALORIES PER MUFFIN: 4 G PROTEIN, 4 G FAT, 29 G CARBOHYDRATE; 149 MG SODIUM; 1 MG CHOLESTEROL

Corn Bread

Of all the recipes that I have taught, this is everyone's favorite. Corn bread is a basic, nurturing food. And even without the butter, it is one of life's simple pleasures. This recipe depends on using the very best cornmeal—stoneground with the germ intact (see Cornmeal box below).

1 cup	cornmeal
1 cup	unbleached white flour
2½ teaspoons	baking powder
½ teaspoon	baking soda

¼ cup	molasses
1¼ cups	buttermilk
⅓ cup	vegetable oil
2	egg whites

1. Combine the dry ingredients until well blended.
2. Whisk together the wet ingredients, then stir them into the dry.
3. Pour into a greased or nonstick 8-inch square pan and bake in a preheated 400 degree F oven for 20 minutes or until the center springs back when pressed. Be careful not to overcook or the corn bread will be heavy and dry. If cooked properly it will be light and moist and will remain that way for a couple of days.

Serves 8

212 CALORIES PER SERVING: 5 G PROTEIN, 10 G FAT, 26 G CARBOHYDRATE;
207 MG SODIUM; 1 MG CHOLESTEROL

Cornmeal

Few people know what true, fresh cornmeal tastes like anymore. When students taste my corn bread in class, they look surprised that something so simple could have such a nutty, rich flavor.

Ground corn goes rancid faster than any other grain, which is why the cornmeal sold in supermarkets has been degerminated. This process removes the germ and all of its oils, flavors, and nutrients. What is left is yellow grit.

The alternative to commercial cornmeal is stoneground cornmeal that still has the germ intact. Natural food stores and gourmet shops are good sources for this. Buy only from a market that keeps its cornmeal refrigerated, or that has a fast turnover and can assure you that the product is fresh. Once home, store the cornmeal in your refrigerator or freezer.

Skillet Drop Bread

The trick to having these little breads come out right is to handle the soft dough as little as possible. The batter will be workable but sticky, so dust your hands with flour before kneading. If more flour is needed (flour varies as to how much moisture it can absorb), add a teaspoon at a time.

1 cup	whole wheat pastry flour
¼ cup	white flour
¼ teaspoon	salt
1 teaspoon	baking soda
½ cup	buttermilk

1. Sift together the dry ingredients, then stir to mix well.
2. Make a well in the center of the dry mixture, pour in the buttermilk, and fold together until a soft ball forms.
3. With floured hands, knead the ball about 5 times, using the heel of your palm, not your fingers.
4. Heat a heavy skillet, preferably well-seasoned and of cast-iron, which will retain heat and cook evenly at a low temperature.
5. Divide the dough into 6 pieces, quickly forming each into the shape of a hamburger patty.
6. Place on the skillet (no shortening is necessary if using cast-iron) and cook for 10 minutes on one side and 7 minutes on the other. Use a flame that is hot enough to brown the bread, but not so hot that it scorches.

Serves 6

94 CALORIES PER SERVING: 4 G PROTEIN, 1 G FAT, 19 G CARBOHYDRATE; 248 MG SODIUM; 1 MG CHOLESTEROL

Biscuits

Hot biscuits, fresh from the oven appeal to just about anyone. These are quick to make and great for unexpected company.

1 cup	unbleached white flour
1 cup	whole wheat pastry flour
1 teaspoon	baking powder
¼ teaspoon	salt
¼ cup	vegetable oil, chilled
¾ cup	buttermilk, still cold from the refrigerator

1. Sift together the dry ingredients and mix well.
2. Make a well in the center of the dry ingredients. Pour in the oil and, using your fingers, quickly mix together until small clumps of dough start to form. Add the buttermilk, again mixing by hand, until a large, rough dough ball forms.
3. Knead the dough in the bowl with the palm of your hand, using about 15 quick strokes.
4. Place dough on a generously floured board and roll out to ½-inch thickness. Cut with a 2-inch biscuit cutter.
5. Place on a nonstick cookie sheet, or one that has been lined with parchment paper and bake in a preheated 450 degree F oven for 10-12 minutes.

Serves 12

118 CALORIES PER BISCUIT: 3 G PROTEIN, 5 G FAT, 16 G CARBOHYDRATE; 89 MG SODIUM; 1 MG CHOLESTEROL

ACCOMPANIMENTS

Condiments, Dips, and Spreads

Neither my body nor my tastebuds appreciate foods swathed in rich sauces, but I do like to enhance the taste of plain foods. When the need is immediate and I don't have time to make something from scratch, I'll use one of the commercially sold products I keep on hand in my pantry. These range from mustards to dressings to sauces.

Before buying commercial brands, I read the labels carefully, looking for those that fit within the guidelines I've set for this book, such as maple syrup-sweetened mustards and chunky chutneys.

In addition to using ready-made products, I make my own condiments, dips, and spreads. Some store well in the refrigerator or freezer, while others should be used more quickly.

Fast and Fresh Cranberry Relish

This sweet-and-sour relish is the perfect accompaniment for both fowl and vegetables. It can be as refreshing in warm weather as it is satisfying in the cool days of fall. Serve it immediately while the flavors are sharp and fresh, or simmer it for 5 minutes to bring out the cranberries and mellow the citrus.

1	juice orange
1	lemon
2 cups	cranberries, sorted and rinsed
8-ounce can	pineapple, packed in its own juices, drained
½ cup	maple syrup

1. Peel the orange and lemon, removing all of the white pith. Slice in half crosswise so the seeds can be removed easily.
2. Put the cranberries, pineapple, citrus, and maple syrup in a food processor fitted with metal blade. Pulse until the mixture is finely chopped but not pureed.
3. If the relish is to be served raw, let it stand at least 1 hour before serving. Otherwise, put it in a saucepan and simmer gently for 5 minutes or until it just starts to thicken.

Serves 6

51 CALORIES PER SERVING: 1 G PROTEIN, 0 G FAT, 13 G CARBOHYDRATE; 1 MG SODIUM; 0 MG CHOLESTEROL

Cranberry and Fruit Chutney

Yes, it *is* time-consuming, and yes, it looks a bit complicated, but it is so much better than canned cranberry relishes. It is even better than most others made from scratch. There are few house gifts more welcome than this chutney. The recipe makes a large quantity because I have friends who demand a jar each autumn. Its uses are unlimited: as a spread for sandwiches or toast, a glaze for roasted poultry, or a mix for chicken salad. This chutney will remain fresh in the refrigerator for at least a month, and can also be frozen.

1	lemon
½ cup	cider vinegar
1½ cups	water
2 cups	honey
¼ teaspoon	ground cardamom
½ teaspoon	ground cinnamon
½ teaspoon	curry powder
¼ teaspoon	ground ginger
¼ teaspoon	allspice
4	navel oranges
6 cups	cranberries, sorted and rinsed
½ cup	golden seedless raisins
½ cup	chopped dried apricots
½ cup	chopped walnuts (optional)

1. Grate the lemon rind, avoiding the white pith under the surface. Juice the lemon and put both the juice and rind into a pot with the vinegar, water, honey, and spices.
2. Grate the rind of 1 of the oranges and put it into the pot.
3. Peel the oranges with a sharp paring knife, and remove the rind and pith. Slice the oranges and add to the pot.
4. Bring this mixture to a boil and cook for 5 minutes. Reduce the heat to a simmer and add 3 cups of the cranberries, the raisins, and apricots. Simmer for 30 minutes or until the chutney starts to thicken.
5. Stir in the remaining cranberries and the walnuts, and cook for another 20 minutes.
6. Allow to cool and then chill.

Yields about 8 cups

84 CALORIES PER 3 TABLESPOONS: 1 G PROTEIN, 1 G FAT, 20 G CARBOHYDRATE; 2 MG SODIUM; 0 MG CHOLESTEROL

Almost Sour Cream

A tablespoon of sour cream contains 25 calories, almost 95% of which comes from fat. As an alternative, I offer this recipe, which is less than 25% fat (15% if you use 1% cottage cheese) and contributes only 12 calories per serving. Because it consists of only 2 ingredients—low-fat cottage cheese and low-fat yogurt—the recipe demands dairy products that are fresh and of the highest quality. There are big differences among products, so try several to find the best.

To achieve a texture like sour cream, it is essential to use a food processor; a blender makes this too thin.

Almost Sour Cream will stay fresh in the refrigerator for up to 4 days. (If some liquid separates out, a quick stir will make it smooth and thick again.) It can be used in tuna salads instead of mayonnaise, baked on top of fish, tossed with vegetables, put on baked potatoes, and spiced up with garlic and onion powders, chives, or parsley.

2 cups	**low-fat cottage cheese**
¼ cup	**low-fat yogurt**

1. Blend the cottage cheese and yogurt in a food processor fitted with metal blade until smooth and without lumps.
2. Serve immediately or store in refrigerator and use as needed.

Yields 2¼ cups

12 CALORIES PER TABLESPOON: 2 G PROTEIN, 0 G FAT, 1 G CARBOHYDRATE; 52 MG SODIUM; 1 MG CHOLESTEROL

Hot! Sauce

Ketchup was never like this!

½	medium onion, chopped (½ cup)
1 teaspoon	vegetable oil
1 cup	water
2 cloves	garlic, minced
3 cups	coarsely chopped tomatoes (red or green, fresh or canned)
2 tablespoons	tomato paste
1 tablespoon	soy sauce
½ teaspoon	ground cumin (or more to taste)
1 teaspoon	ground coriander
½ to 1 teaspoon	cayenne pepper (or to taste)
6 drops	hot pepper sauce
½ tablespoon	chili powder
2 tablespoons	red wine

1. Sauté the onion in the oil and enough of the water to keep the onion from sticking. Cook until the onion is softened, then add the garlic and sauté for 2 more minutes.
2. Add the rest of the water, along with the other ingredients. Simmer for at least 30 minutes. (Since flavors improve with long, slow cooking, simmer longer if you have the time, but be careful with the hot spices, which get stronger as the sauce cooks.) Adjust your seasonings after the first half hour.

Yields 3½ cups

9 CALORIES PER 2 TABLESPOONS: 1 G PROTEIN, 1 G FAT, 2 G CARBOHYDRATE; 79 MG SODIUM; 0 MG CHOLESTEROL

Curry Orange Dip

Serve as an appetizer with fresh fruit, fresh vegetables, or crackers.

1 pound	low-fat cottage cheese
¼ cup	low-fat yogurt
¼ teaspoon	lemon juice
2 tablespoons	frozen orange juice concentrate
1 teaspoon	curry powder

¼ teaspoon	ground cardamom
¹⁄₁₆ teaspoon	cayenne pepper

1. Puree all of the ingredients in a food processor fitted with metal blade until the texture is smooth and creamy.
2. Chill before serving.

Yields 2½ cups

21 CALORIES PER 2 TABLESPOONS: 3 G PROTEIN, 1 G FAT, 1 G CARBOHYDRATE; 94 MG SODIUM; 1 MG CHOLESTEROL

Hummus with Tahini

Use this as a dip or as a sandwich filling. The combination of chick-peas and tahini makes it a complete protein and a nutritious food.

2 cloves	garlic
2 cups	cooked chick-peas
⅓ cup	tahini
3 tablespoons	lemon juice
⅓ cup	water, or chick-pea cooking liquid (don't use the liquid from canned chick peas; it contains too much salt and usually tastes too much like the can)
½ teaspoon	salt
⅛ teaspoon	cayenne pepper

1. Mince the garlic in a food processor fitted with metal blade.
2. Add the remaining ingredients and puree until smooth, using additional liquid if needed.

Serves 8

68 CALORIES PER SERVING: 4 G PROTEIN, 1 G FAT, 11 G CARBOHYDRATE; 136 MG SODIUM; 0 MG CHOLESTEROL

Tofu Sandwich Spread

Don't let the long list of ingredients intimidate you. This recipe can be whipped up quickly in a food processor, or done by hand in little time.

1 pound	firm tofu
1 tablespoon	lemon juice
1 tablespoon	cider vinegar
½ teaspoon	honey
2 teaspoons	soy sauce
1 tablespoon	corn oil
⅛ teaspoon	freshly ground pepper
4 drops	hot pepper sauce
1 teaspoon	dried dill
¼ teaspoon	onion powder
1 tablespoon	minced fresh parsley
1	carrot

1. Combine the tofu and all but the last 2 ingredients in a food processor fitted with metal blade. Process until semi-chunky.
2. Add the parsley, processing only 1 or 2 seconds to prevent the spread from turning green.
3. Replace the metal blade with the grater blade and process the carrot into the work bowl.
4. Empty the contents into a container and stir until well blended.

Serves 8

64 CALORIES PER SERVING: 5 G PROTEIN, 4 G FAT, 3 G CARBOHYDRATE; 93 MG SODIUM; 0 MG CHOLESTEROL

Index